UNBROKEN
IDENTITY

The tears, trials and triumph
of the King's daughter

BECKY IBRAHIM

UNBROKEN
IDENTITY

The tears, trials and triumph
of the King's daughter

BECKY IBRAHIM

The events and conversations in this book have been set
down to the best of the author's recollection, although some
names and details have been changed to protect the privacy
of individuals.

Printed in the Federal Republic of Nigeria.
First Printing, 2020.

ISBN 978-978-983-296-5 (Print)
ISBN 978-978-983-296-5 (Electronic)

Becky Ibrahim
www.beckyibrahim.com

All scripture references are taken from the New King James Version of the
Holy Bible. Where otherwise, the conventional acronym of the translation
is stated.

Designed & Printed by

www.maxximo.com
+234 814 293 2770

To my heavenly father, Jesus, who has blessed me with His love and identity. In Him alone my hope is found.

To my loving husband of no regret, Akeem, in whom I am well pleased. Your love and support are invaluable.

To my son, Othniel, for being the star that you are and your love for God.

To my son, Jamiel, for being an amazing treasure, I thank God always for you.

To my son, Haniel, for the doggedness you bring to things; you inspire me.

ACKNOWLEDGEMENTS

So many persons have contributed in many ways to birthing this book. It is impossible for me to mention everyone by name, but I want you to know, I appreciate you all for the effort and for the encouragement you have given me in the course of making this book happen.

Specifically, my appreciation goes to my husband, Akeem Ibrahim, for your constant support, proof-reading and deep insights to birth this book. Your love is my strength.

To Pastor Afolabi Ibrahim, my brother, your effort in tirelessly proof-reading and editing of the manuscript is deeply appreciated.

To Richard Okere, thank you for your dedication.

To Sam Gaza, your commitment to editing is so exceptional.

To the entire Pwatee's staff, you are simply the best.

Lastly, to my mum, your love and prayers will not go unrewarded.

God bless and keep you all!

CONTENTS

FOREWORD

The author of this excellent book, Becky Ibrahim, ventilates the meaning of unbroken, or complete, identity and how it is important for every woman and man to fit into what God intends them to be. She elaborates the fact that God is our Father and King, and that makes up for the negative effects of the deficiency of fathers in our society today, which are numerous. In this epoch when many fathers and husbands are either physically or emotionally absent in the lives of their daughters, wives or family altogether, this treatise, I believe, is an antidote to this anomaly.

The author, a woman blessed with wisdom and great insight in God's word, draws upon her walk with God of almost 3 decades to enumerate the fact that the cardinal desire of our Creator was a family of sons and daughters on whose love and trustful devotion His heart could feed, and in turn pour His endless love on as He fellowships with them every day. This piece reveals the efficacy of allowing God to have a Father's place in our hearts, and not a guest's. In my sincere opinion, this book is a masterful revelation of God's love toward us.

In today's hurting world, the content of this book will meet the needs of every downtrodden person spiritually, emotionally and psychologically as the author stresses the fact that the Lord cares deeply for you and He can be totally trusted as you cast that pain upon Him now. Without any doubt, this book provides solution to crushed relationships and broken fellowship. It will help you discover your identity and embolden you to ditch the mark of defeat.

Reading through the pages of this book you will encounter nuggets that will revolutionize your concept of God as a Father to you. The book is a direct expression of what Jesus said in John 14:23-

Jesus answered and said to him, "If anyone loves Me, he will keep My word; and My Father will love him, and We will come to him and make Our home with him.

More so, it is, beyond doubt, an articulation of Romans 8:15-

For you did not receive the spirit of bondage again to fear, but you received the Spirit of adoption by whom we cry out, "Abba, Father."

The book elegantly debunks the many lies the devil has told us, as well as our struggles with guilt and feelings of hopelessness, while asserting the brutal reality of how Jesus has given us victory entrenched deeply in who we are in Him. It will surely make us come to our senses as recorded in Luke 15:17, NIV-

When he came to his senses, he said, 'How many of my father's hired servants have food to spare, and here I am starving to death!

I trust God that every woman and every believer who reads this book will experience healing in all areas of their lives in Jesus name!

I personally recommend this book for every believer; I encourage you to peruse each chapter of this volume prayerfully and be blessed in Jesus' name!

Evang. Gboyega SHITTA
June 2020

AUTHOR'S NOTE

The Holy Spirit has inspired me to write this book as a tool for the healing of many, especially women. Many women are carrying baggage that no one knows about – sometimes even their husbands. They wallow in defeat, clueless about how to gain solution to their deep, hidden sense of rejection, lack of love, and depression. Many women were abused while growing up. Sure, the specifics and dynamics differ, but they are abuses, nonetheless. Sadly, we live in a society that almost deliberately tries to muzzle the woman from voicing out. Women are repressed even while being abused in different ways. They suffer, yet they can't speak up. They are threatened to keep mute. And where there is no direct threat, society already threatens them by its aloofness towards the plight of women. So, they ask themselves, "Who will believe me if I speak out? Will anyone even listen to me when it will be my words against my predator's?" It is an endless cycle of seeking love and getting rejected over and again.

Like the women, many men, too, suffered emotional and physical abuses as boys, some even endured sexual abuse from people they trusted and looked up to. Many grew up without true fathers and lacked positive role models. They neither experienced true love nor learnt to give and receive the affection that comes with it. Hence, many suffer from the same identity crises that their female counterparts suffer from, albeit often conveniently masked under the guise of masculinity. They yearn for love and fulfilment, and resort to various vices to plug the void they feel in their souls.

Maybe you should consider seeking this love elsewhere than you currently are. But first, don't judge yourself for desiring to be loved. Your feelings and longings are genuine and legitimate. God put them there. He created you last, after all of creation had been put in place, so that you can enjoy all the good that He had already furnished the world with. So, you must not allow the devil to sway you away from all that your wonderful Father has stored up for you to enjoy – the fundamental of them being *love*.

A woman, especially, craves to be loved. She naturally gravitates towards wherever she finds love, even if it is a guise. However, as humans, we were raised and taught to look for love in the secondary places, not from the source of love Himself – God. Outside God, you cannot find true love – the kind you seek. Therefore, this book is a tool for healing to that lady or man reading this, who has been beaten, broken and battered by the vicissitudes of life. This book is for the woman who is tired of the mess society has tossed at her. For that man or woman who, like Gideon, should be a deliverer but is hiding in shame, contented to have just enough to feed on. I trust God that an end has come to that ordeal as you read through the pages of this book.

Please note that, for the sake of simplicity, I have hereafter, intentionally chosen to refer to the female gender as a generalisation for all humans, except where mentioning both genders will enhance clarity. This is to avoid the encumbrance of having to continually refer to both genders separately in the same sentence.

INTRODUCTION

The ancient story of Gideon the son of Joash (Judges 6-8) is one I think about quite often, especially as it pertains to the subject of self-identity. I wonder how many people in our world today, like Gideon, are living as shadows of themselves, unaware of God's tremendous deposits inside them. How many people live as peasants instead of the royalties that we all are in Christ? How many live every day oblivious of their identity in Christ?

For a long time, Israel had unrepentantly lived contrary to God's precepts and commandments to them until He withdrew His hedge of protection around them and the Medianites began to lord over them. For seven years, the elect people of God became victims and subjects to a heathen nation. The Medianites did whatever they wished to Israel and no one could confront them. In fact, all the Israelites knew to do was hide, run and try to barely survive. Their fear kept them as slaves.

What is most disturbing is the fact that the man who had the divine mandate to bring about salvation for the entire nation of Israel was also hiding and living in fear. He didn't even know what his divine assignment on earth was. He too, like everyone else, hid in the rocks to thresh flour and hide it from their oppressors who were determined to impoverish and starve the nation by destroying their crops. Gideon did not know who he was, so he lived like a victim.

> *Do not call conspiracy everything this people call a conspiracy;*
> *do not fear what they fear, and do not dread it.*
> – Isaiah 8:12, NIV

Ignorance of who you are by divine design makes you a victim of life's negative circumstances. It makes you vulnerable to every curveball that life throws at you. You lack a sense of identity. You live a clueless life, only groping in the dark as each day passes, with no idea of where your life is headed and what exactly you are supposed to do with the daily gifts of 24 hours that God generously gives to you. As such, you waste every bit of it – every day. The only thing you are certain of about your life is the fact that you are confused, clueless, frustrated, and most times depressed.

I have been there. I know that place you are right now and fully understand how it feels. I have felt worthless and so depressed before that I contemplated suicide. I even came close to packing up my things and leaving my husband and two kids when our marriage was seven years old. But thank God for His love! His love set me free. That is why you have this book in your hand right now. It was written to take you through a journey of self-discovery and a fulfilling life in Christ hereafter. Your life can and will be sweet again regardless of what your past looks like and despite your present circumstances.

Maybe you are like Gideon who had gotten used to his situation and couldn't see a possible way out of the grip of his oppressors. He had resigned to his circumstances as his fate, so much that he totally discountenanced and ignored the angel's words when he called him a mighty man of valour. Gideon pretended to not have heard that and rather poured out his grievance to God for forsaking them onto the wickedness of the Medianites. However, what he failed to realize in that instance was that the words he ignored held the key to the freedom he desperately needed for himself and his people. In fact, *he* was the solution to the problem he was lamenting over and that phrase he pretended to not have heard was his empowerment for the call of destiny upon his life. The angel had come to activate it!

I have been privileged of God to have been led through a process that brought healing to my soul after a long string of tumultuous, unstable and traumatic childhood experiences that left me wondering who I was and why I had to go through all of those pains and heartaches. Looking back, I can connect the dots and I am grateful for every experience: the good, the bad and the ugly. They were all pieces of the puzzle that created the woman that I am today.

In this book, I want to share bits and pieces of my story with you: how I got broken and how God picked up the many scattered pieces of my life and used them to build the whole, complete, unbroken and "proud" woman that I am today. Through the revelation of His great love for me as His daughter, God gave me a deep sense of identity, purpose and ability to love – first myself, then others. Now He has impressed in my heart to share these truths with you and I am deeply grateful for the privilege and I trust that these truths will bless and transform you as they did me.

The thrust of this book is to practically show you that irrespective of what crippling circumstances life has doled you – whether in the past or present, you are the King's heir, and your identity in Him is still intact. Your circumstances in life are not the determinants of your identity, but who the King – your Father – says you are. As such, no matter what your past or present says or looks like, you have an *unbroken identity* in Christ! This book is solely intended to reveal to you, or remind you, that you are whole and complete in Him. So, 'Unbroken Identity' in this context refers to your wholeness and completeness in Christ your Lord, the King.

Do not discountenance the words contained in the following pages. I am convinced that this book is a tool that the Holy Spirit will use to bring healing to your heart and give you a peek into His divine call upon your life. He will also empower you to become that *mighty woman* or *man of valour* who will confront and defeat the oppressors of your life, your family, your community and the many destinies God has tied to yours.

While I was starting to collate my thoughts for this book, I shared my story with several young ladies in a group and nearly all of them had the "I can't believe it" look on their faces. It was a look of surprise stemming from the fact that my life in the present doesn't look anything like the past I was painting to them by the story I was sharing. However, as I progressed, I saw their faces brighten one after another and knew that they had found answers through the story and lessons I shared. I pray that that will be your testimony after flipping through the pages in this book. May the light of God's word empower you to enlighten and brighten people's world around you.

Chapter

ONE

THE KING

Recently, I saw a meme that shows a little boy asking his father what it means to be a man. The father responded by saying, "A man is an adult who protects and provides for his family". Then the little boy, who was apparently impressed and having a point of reference for his understanding of his father's reply said, "When I grow up, I want to be a man like mom!"

Funny as that may sound, it underscores the regrettable fact that many fathers are absent in their children's lives. Sadly, this often applies to physical, emotional, and psychological absence. Many fathers are only figureheads: masculine humans who get married, have children, then work their lives out to make food available to the family, while losing sight of the negative impact that their absence is having on their children's growth and development. Any child who grows without a present father hardly ever grows whole and complete. A significant chunk of their wholeness as children, and even adults, is chopped away. I know this for a fact because that was my experience growing up. I grew up without a father in my life, and that broke me – especially because of the many other ill experiences that were offshoots of his absence.

I lost my biological father early in life. I was only 4 years old. As the custom was, all my father's property was carted away by relatives, leaving us – my mom and five children – with nothing. I couldn't understand his absence, hence, from a tender age, the love of a parent had been strongly questioned in my mind; more so because I didn't grow up with my mother either. When I turned 6, I was sent to live with an uncle in Lagos, more than a thousand miles away from anything or anyone I was familiar with. I barely saw my uncle during the week except on Sundays because of the nature of his work. Chiefly, the reason was that he wasn't awake when I left for school in the morning and he was hardly back home when I went to bed at night. So, I never had the opportunity to enjoy a father-daughter relationship. I never understood what fatherhood meant or what it means to have a father in your life as a girl-child. I didn't experience the affection, the fellowship, the instruction and guidance, etc. that comes from a father. I never had that relationship, even though I innocently yearned earnestly for it.

I was like the little child in the meme I talked about – maybe even worse, because in my case I didn't have a true parent figure in my life for the most part. I was torn between several adults who, mostly, chipped away a part of my being. It was a trail of woes, one after another.   This made me a weakling, a no-good; beautiful but victimized, tender, naïve and pained.

I grew up among adults, with scanty presence of other children. And, contrary to what you may expect, I wasn't spoiled with or enjoying all the attention from everyone around, I experienced the opposite. I got attention quite alright, but it was the upturned and corrosive type of attention. Everyone always appeared to want something from me – something I couldn't or shouldn't have given. I was framed, accused and distrusted. I was physically, verbally and emotionally abused. I was deliberately tortured in different ways. I was assaulted. I cannot even begin to count the many times I contemplated suicide, for the sheer measure of rejection that life had meted on me. I wondered why. What did I do wrong? Why did it have to be me? When will it all end? Will it even ever end? A once happy and energetic little girl grew into a bitter, broken and docile teenager. I remember before going to Lagos how we used to go fishing in nearby streams. We would climb trees to pluck fruits, play under the rain and so on. It was so much fun. All these faded away and I was turned to a dispirited girl without love, care, attention or affection. And this filtered its way into my adult life, my relationships, and ultimately my marriage – and nearly broke it at different times.

I never thought of or perceived the term 'father' as a relational concept. Instead, I saw a father as the male figure in a house, responsible for providing for the needs of the home and everyone in it. However, that ideology got crushed every time my material needs were not met. So, I struggled with a fluctuating understanding or interpretation of fatherhood. An incident that is a case in point here is one I had while I was still a second year Junior Secondary School student at Federal Government College, Ijanikin, Lagos State, Nigeria. One day, one of my classmates walked up to me and asked if my father was alive. Of course, I answered, with a passionate smile on my face and feeling grateful that he was. At the time, I considered my uncle as my dad since I had been with him since age six, and I had no recollection of my biological father. Unfortunately for me, nothing prepared me for her response to my giggly answer – the reason she asked the question in the first place. While I wondered in my mind why she asked the question, she responded: "Wow! My father will never let me wear torn clothes and worn out shoes." Yes, those were her exact words. Then she giggled, turned and walked away.

My heart was pierced, shattered by her words and I was deeply pained, perhaps more than I had ever been before that time because she was right. I had deficiencies in nearly everything, but no one ever confronted me or rubbed it in my face like she did on that fateful day. At the time, I had only one pair of uniform, which were torn; my shoes were worn out; my hair was in bad shape, because I had lost much of it due to neglect. I didn't have money, didn't have provisions. It was evident that I had nothing to prove that I was someone's daughter. I had to depend solely on school food all the time, which sometimes I didn't get enough of.

It was in that moment and for the first time, I really thought about my biological father. Who was he? Would he have looked out for me if he was alive? Would I be going through these if he was alive? Is it because I am not my uncle's biological daughter that I was neglected and given the sense of not being valued? I asked countless questions and got no answers. To make matters worse, whenever I brought up my needs at home, it was as if I was asking for too much; I was met with harsh responses. So, overtime I learnt not to speak up. I resorted to managing anything I was given without complaining or asking for anything more.

My uncle, who had become my surrogate father, failed to fulfil the perfect role of a father in my life. He did his best, and for that I am forever grateful, but he was limited in his understanding of the place of a father in the life of his daughter and his importance in shaping her overall outlook on life. This underscores man's weakness and inability to express the full potential of true love. Mankind is a limited entity.

Man, especially when he is not in Christ, is incapable of expressing true, selfless love. By default, every human being is selfish and thinks only of themselves and what is convenient for them. Only God can truly love in the purest form of love and its finest expression. God is love personified. And He demonstrated His love for us when we were most undeserving of it by sending His Son to die for us in order to reconcile us to Himself, cleansed from our sins.

God did not only create the world; He loved His creation. And you and I are His creation, so He loves us infinitely. Unfortunately, this is what many fathers in our world today fail to do. For them, fatherhood ends with donating sperm to an open and willing female recipient who utilizes it to produce a baby after nine months. That's all. Or if they care to go further, they stick around to provide food, clothes, shelter, pay school fees and all. Am I discounting these? Far from it! They are a vital part of fatherly duties. What I am saying, however, is that it doesn't end there; there is much more that is required if that child will grow up wholesome and maximize their God-ordained purpose for coming to earth.

A Silent Epidemic

Let me show you just how terrible and perplexing this absentee-fatherhood problem is and how deeply into our societal fabric it has eaten. According to fathers.com:[1] "If it were classified as a disease, fatherlessness would be an epidemic worthy of attention as a national emergency."

Carefully consider the data below (for the USA):
- An estimated 24.7 million children live in a home without the physical presence of a father. Millions more have dads who are physically present, but emotionally absent.
- 71% of High School dropouts are from fatherless homes.
- 71% of teenage pregnancies happen with kids from homes with absent fathers.

- 85% of children with behavioural disorders have their fathers absent in their lives.
- 90% of homeless and runaway children have absent fathers.
- 63% of youth suicide victims come from fatherless homes.
- 85% of youths in prison are victims of fatherlessness.
- Children are four times more likely to live in poverty if the father is not around.[2]
- At the root of kids' academic problems is the lack of a relationship with their father.
- Without the father present, girls are four times more likely to get pregnant as teenagers.
- Individuals from father-absent homes are 79% more likely to carry guns and deal drugs than peers living with their fathers.[3]
- The absence of a biological father contributes to increased risk of child maltreatment.
- Men with absent fathers are more likely to become absent fathers themselves.

Enough! Let's get a little breath of fresh air, shall we?
- Involved dads improve their children's overall emotional and social well-being.
- Children with involved dads are less likely to be mistreated.
- Children who live with their dads do better in school.
- Teen boys who live with involved dads are less likely to carry guns and deal drugs.

Sadly, data for the fatherlessness problem in Nigeria is scarce. However, it is an epidemic all the same. It is estimated that 63% of African children have fathers who are either absent or deceased.[4]

Father-absenteeism manifests in different ways. Sometimes, it is outright physical absence where the father has little or no contact with his child. At other times, it is an emotional absence where the father lives in the same house with the child but is not involved in their lives outside the provision of basic needs. Yet, there are fathers who don't only live with their children and are emotionally absent, but they go further to abuse the children – physically, emotionally, or psychologically. Painfully, this is a growing menace in our world.

With a dearth of actual data, I will risk asserting that, in Nigeria, we tend to have more of emotionally absent fathers than physically absent fathers. This is based on my personal observation, though, and I don't have data to prove it. Notwithstanding, my point is that we have a problem on our hands that we must awaken to. Enough of the disempowering mind-set that it is women who raise children. That belief must have its source in hell, because it has successfully bred half-baked children who turned out as imbalanced adults in Africa.

How can a parent not know what class their child is in per time? Why would a parent not know what school the kids attend or forget their birthday or current age? Why would he be unaware of their favourite colour, best food, interests, likes and dislikes, etc.? If you ever find a parent like this, they are simply absent from their child's life.

My Editor once shared with me how his dad once asked him, back in high school, what class he was at the time. He answered but wondered for a long time afterward what kind of father wouldn't remember his child's class when he is the one paying the fees. What his teenage mind didn't realize at the time is that he wasn't alone. Some other children had it even worse. It is a silent, global epidemic!

According to feminine.com.ng, here are some ways absent fathers hurt their children:[5]

- Being an emotionally absent father makes your children hardened. They lack feelings and find it hard to show emotions.
- Children with absent fathers suffer increased rates of depression and anxiety.
- These children suffer decreased education levels and increased drop-out rates.
- These children have serious relationship issues and are more likely to divorce their spouses.
- These children find it hard to get and keep jobs.
- Some of these children become addicted to drugs and abuse substances.
- They have social and mental behavioural issues. They find it hard to interact with others.
- Some of them have anger issues that can be traced back to not having their fathers around.

This is simply sad!

A Father's Role

Fathers play a role in every child's life that cannot be filled by others. This role can have a large impact on a child and help shape him or her into the person they become.[6]

A father's role is divine and fundamental to the total growth and wellbeing of their children. They lay the foundations of discipline, morality, worth, respect, excellence, healthy relationships, courtesy, emotional and mental health, physical and emotional security, inner strength, spirituality, etc. Studies have shown that when fathers are affectionate and supportive, it greatly affects their children's cognitive and social development. It also instils an overall sense of well-being and self-confidence.[7]

The absence of a father from the life of his children opens them up to abuse and misdirection. Sons easily turn wayward and go astray, while daughters become fair game to callous men who will seek to take advantage of them. As I will share in more details in subsequent chapters, this was my plight, growing up. The absence of a father in my life opened me up to all kinds of ills. I was exposed and vulnerable to wicked men, starting from right inside my home (my uncle's house). It was the most excruciating of experiences. These men who lived as staff in the house saw the loophole created by the absence of my uncle (now father) and leeched on it to exercise their evil enterprises. But all praise to my King-Father who, though I did not know Him at the time, still preserved me.

A child obtains his or her identity from their father. The father is the first representation of who the child should be in future. They derive their confidence and sense of worth, first from their father, before any other person who may come into their lives. To the child, a father epitomizes strength and power. He symbolizes authority, protection and provision. He is a mentor. So, a child that is deprived of having a true, loving and present father in their life will struggle much in life, especially with finding their self-identity, even if they escape exposure to harmful experiences. And this goes beyond having a father living with them in the same house. I am talking about *conscious presence*. As we have established, some fathers are present at their homes, yet absent from their children's lives because they fail to establish connection founded on expressive and disciplined love. This equals absence. If you are a father reading this, please don't fall into this hole where the devil wants you; it will have debilitating effects on your children as they grow – emotionally, psychologically, socially, educationally, spiritually and all.

In my case, I lived in the same house with my father, yet, for the most part, he had no idea what terrible mess I was confronted with right under his roof. And, in few instances, the hurts came from him.

Introducing the Father of Fathers

Now, having dealt much with the debilitating effects of having an absent father, as well as the role of a father in their child's life, let me introduce to you the *Father of all fathers: God.* He is the author and epitome of true fatherly love.

> *For God so loved the world, that He gave His only begotten Son,*
> *that whosoever believes in Him should not perish but*
> *have everlasting life.*
> – John 3:16

In the scripture above, what particularly stands out for me is that "God *so* loved the world..." I just can't get enough of that clause. It literally sends goose chills rippling through my skin each time I meditate upon that fact. God loves *me*. God loves *you*. I hope you believe that. More importantly, God didn't just love us, as in lip service; He demonstrated His love for us by giving up His most priced treasure – His Son Jesus – to prove that love to us by laying down His life for our sins. What an amazing gesture! What an amazing character of God! His love for us, for the world at large, for humanity, was so demonstrated through Jesus. It was the ultimate price. And through our acceptance of the sacrifice of Jesus through His shameful death on the cross, burial and resurrection, we have entered God's eternal love.

> *Behold, what manner of love the Father has bestowed on us,*
> *That we should be called children of God!...*
> – 1 John 3:1

Irrespective of what your experience with your earthly father was or is, I want you to know that *God, the King of the universe is your Father.* That is what the Bible says. And He is a perfect Father. His love is pure, present, sacrificial, and everlasting.

The Fatherhood of the King

God, the Creator of all things and King over heaven and the entire universe, is our Father! Did you hear that? I'll repeat: God, more than everything else that He is and represents to us, is our Father. And He readied Himself for Fatherhood long before we were created. He may be judge to the world and God to the sinner, but I choose to refer to Him as Father. That is who He is and will ever be to me and to everyone who identifies with Him.

For you did not receive the spirit of bondage again to fear, but you received the Spirit of adoption by whom we cry out, "Abba, Father."
– Romans 8:15

According as He hath chosen us in Him before the foundation of the world, that we should be holy and without blame before Him in love.
– Ephesians 1:4

God's original purpose for creating Adam and Eve was to cultivate a family of sons and daughters of the great King of the universe. And He placed us on earth, a territorial extension of the King's kingdom, ruled by His heirs. But unfortunately, man messed up and lost that eternal privilege. We lost our place of sonship in God and came under the rulership of Satan through disobedience. We became victims of the devil's wickedness. But God had foreseen this, and from the great depth of His eternal love for humanity, He provided an escape plan even before the sin was committed. He slew the Lamb before the foundations of the world were laid (1 Peter 1:19-20). Little wonder the Bible says there is no greater love than the love Christ showed to us by dying on the cross for our sins. God prepared for fatherhood ahead of time.

Who is a King?

A king is a ruler who has a province, a jurisdiction of influence called kingdom'. The word 'kingdom' comes from two words: 'king' and domain'. That means a kingdom is a king's domain of influence and rulership.

Today's world, mostly operating democratic system of governance, doesn't help us to understand the concept of kingship. If anything, it skews our understanding instead. Democracy preaches and practices equality of all citizens before the eyes of the law governing a society and people. That is a very good thing. I believe it is the best system of governance that our present world needs for all people to have equal opportunities to reach for the best of themselves in life.

However, in distant human history, the then world was made up of clusters of kingdoms ruled by kings who had absolute responsibility for the wellbeing, protection and prosperity of their subjects, who in turn were loyal to their king.

When a king is absent from his domain, either physically or by abdication of responsibility, his kingdom becomes vulnerable and an easy prey for the enemy. Remember the story of how King David left for battle with his army and returned to find the city spoiled by the Amalekites and their wives and children carted away as slaves? (1 Samuel 30:1-18). Therefore, we have a King-Father who is ever present in our lives. He never sleeps nor slumbers. He never leaves us nor forsakes us. He is omnipresent, so He sees and knows everything happening everywhere in the universe at the same time. So, you have no need to fear that He may be somewhere at a time when you most need Him. He is ever present with His children and cares very deeply for us.

The Father's Love

For the Father himself loves you. He loves you because you love me and have believed that I came from God.
–John 16:27, GNB

What a joy to know that the Father Himself loves me. This means that irrespective of all the burdens and cares of life that I may ever be confronted with, the Father *loves* me. Whatever the heartache, whatever the burden, whatever the secret grief, the heart of my great Father-God yearns for me. This gives me undaunted strength to press on when reasons to fail are glaring. This is my fuel for holding on to faith and trusting Him for deliverance from whatever challenges I may be faced with per time. It should do the same for you. Trust me; all you will ever need to walk in perpetual victory from now on is the revelation of God's love for you.

The primal dream of the Creator-God was a family of sons and daughters on whose love and loyal devotion His heart could feed (2 Corinthians 6:18). His purpose was to have sons and daughters that He would pour His infinite love on and fellowship with every day. Thus, He desires to live with His children continually (John 14:23). He does not want to simply be a guest in our homes; He wants to have a Father's place in our lives and hearts (Revelations 3:20). He wants to be part of our daily lives and all we do. He desires that we commune with Him so He can guide and lead us on to victory and success every day (2 Corinthians 13:14). He will show us how to avoid misfortune and where to find opportunities and favour that will lift us (2 Timothy 4:17).

Therefore, Jesus made us a precious promise that He and the Father will come and make their home with us (John 14:23). What else could be better and sweeter? They would become our burden-bearer, comforter, and we would depend on their wisdom and protection in all of life's hard struggles.

The Father-God yearns over us with tenderness. He craves fellowship and partnership with us. And consequently, He demonstrates His love in His power. His power demonstrates His unbiased provision and protection through His love for us. The gospel conveys God's love and power to us. Anyone who has believed the gospel of Christ has received the love of God and can walk in the same.

Behold what manner of love the Father has given unto us, that we should be called the sons of God.
– John 3:1

I am proud of the good news! It is God's powerful way of saving all people who have faith, whether they are Jews or Gentiles.
– Romans 1:16, (CEV)

God deposited His love in our hearts at the instance of new birth and that brought us into a relationship with Him. God did this all by Himself. He did that so that He can relate with the believer only in love. Love is the highest expression of the person of our Father-God.

And we have known and believed the love that God has for us. God is love, and he who abides in love abides in God, and God in him.
Love has been perfected among us in this: that we may have boldness in the day of judgment; because as He is, so are we in this world.
There is no fear in love; but perfect love casts out fear, because fear involves torment. But he who fears has not been made perfect in love.
We love Him because He first loved us.
– I John 4:16-19

God's utmost desire is for us to gain comprehensive knowledge of His love so that it forms the basis of our faith. The scripture cited above is not so much about the love we have for God, but the love that God has for us. *God is love, and he who dwells in love dwells in God, and God in him.*

Powerful! In other words, if you do not have the love of God resident inside you and exuding through you to the world around you, then God is not in you and you are not in Him. There is no hate in God.

Believers, in this generation, we need to give ourselves wholly to the love of God. It's an aberration to see believers who do not walk in love; rather they resort to bitterness, anger, hate and strife.

But I say to you, love your enemies, bless those who curse you, do good to those who hate you, and pray for those who spitefully use you and persecute you, that you may be sons of your Father in heaven; for He makes His sun rise on the evil and on the good, and sends rain on the just and on the unjust.
— Matthew 5:44-45

God's instruction is to love our enemies and do good to them that curse us and spitefully use and persecute us. He says that is the way to be like our heavenly Father. That means love is the bedrock for living and functioning in the true nature of who we are.

When you received the gospel, what you received was the love of God. Then you were born again; that is, born of the Spirit. And the Holy Ghost who is given to us sheds the love of God abroad in our hearts. So, you are born of God, which is *born of love*. It is therefore crucial to learn how to walk in and manifest this love nature we now have, through a comprehensive knowledge of the love of God, which is in Christ Jesus. The revelation of the love of God gives us the understanding that we are exactly as Christ is today. Hallelujah!

The key to faith and spiritual boldness is the understanding of the love of God in your heart; and boldness is needed to function with the things of the Spirit. Without boldness, you cannot effectively preach the gospel and execute other kingdom responsibilities that we have been assigned. Boldness is a necessity for ruling and reigning on earth and in God's kingdom.

> *Now when they saw the boldness of Peter and John, and perceived that they were uneducated and untrained men, they marvelled. And they realized that they had been with Jesus.*
> – Acts 4:13

Peter and John had been soaked in the revelation of God's eternal love for them as revealed in Jesus, and there was no stopping them from conquering their world.

Dear child of God, I want you to know – more than anything else – that God, the King of the Universe *is* your Father. So, if you have ever suffered rejection or the many other consequences of the absence of love in your life, I want you to absorb this truth right now: the truth that *The King is your Father*, and He loves you with an everlasting love. Nothing will change that. That's your past, present and future reality!

Chapter

TWO

HIS DAUGHTER

One story in the Bible that always speaks warmly to my heart is the parable of the lost son, or the prodigal son, as it is mostly called.

Jesus continued: "there was a man who had two sons.
The younger son said to his father, 'Father, give me my share of the estate.'
So, he divided his property between them.
Not long after that, the younger son got together all he had, set off for a
distant country and there squandered his wealth in wild living.
After he had spent everything, there was a severe famine
in that whole country, and he began to be in need.
So, he went and hired himself out to a citizen of that country,
who sent him to his fields to feed pigs.
He longed to fill his stomach with the pods that the pigs were eating,
but no one gave him anything.
"WHEN HE CAME TO HIS SENSES, he said, 'How many of my father's
hired servants have food to spare, and here I am starving to death!
I will set out and go back to my father and say to him: father,
I have sinned against heaven and against you.
I am no longer worthy to be called your son
make me like one of your hired servants.'
So, he got up and went to his father, "But while he was still a long way off, his
father saw him and was filled with compassion for him; he ran to his son, threw
his arms around him and kissed him.

"The son said to him, 'Father, I have sinned against you. I am no longer worthy to be called your son.'
"But the father said to his servants, 'Quick! Bring the best robe and put it on him. Put a ring on his finger and sandals on his feet.
Bring the fattened calf and kill it. Let's have a feast and celebrate. For this son of mine was dead and is alive again; he was lost and is found.' So, they began to celebrate."
– Luke 15:11-24 (NIV)

This story holds a lot of lessons for us as God's children, especially for the woman who has been beaten and battered by life's harsh whips. Whether you contributed to the many troubles you have faced so far in life or not, God has never stopped loving you – and He can never stop. He loved you from start, long before you were born, with an everlasting love. He created you, as *an eternal excellency, the joy of many generations* (Isaiah 60:15). You are special to God, the eternal King (1 Timothy4:17); so much that He tattooed you on the palm of His hand so that He can never forget you. Though you pass through the valley of the shadow of death, He is right there with you.

The lost son's father in Jesus' story never stopped loving the son – not even for a day. Sadly, the boy's foolishness brought his predicament upon him. He made the stupid mistake of leaving his father's wealth, love and protection.

Maybe you're saying to yourself: "But unlike the prodigal son, I didn't do anything to warrant the hardship I have suffered through life." All you did was to love your man selflessly and sacrificially, yet he mistreated you at every chance he got. You were an innocent and naïve little girl, yet that uncle abused and violated you. All you wanted to do was be an outgoing girl, as an escape from the turbulent childhood you had as a result of your parents' unstable marriage, but you ended up as a teenage mother and everyone seized the opportunity to slice off a piece of your soul through mockery, slander, and wicked criticisms. Like everyone else, you believed you had the right to dream and to pursue those dreams, but that superior in the office just wouldn't let you thrive. He was mean to you at every opportunity and eventually orchestrated your sack, leaving you stranded and unable to meet your basic needs, just because you wouldn't give in to his demands to violate your chastity. What did you do wrong? Why is life so unfriendly and cruel towards you? Did you commit a crime by being born into the world as a woman?

Those questions you ask are legitimate and honest. I feel you, sister. And I am all too familiar with them. I asked countless questions for many years, too. Thanks to the Holy Spirit, He showed me answers that liberated me over time.

The first thing that must happen to you is to "come to your senses" like the lost son did. That implies self-awareness. A realization of who you are is what will empower you to seek the best and permanent solution to your many troubles. Many women, as a result of the challenges and neglect they have faced in life, have resigned to ill fate in their hearts and have quit trying for solutions. They are famished, drained, used up, they languish in hurt, pain, emotional instability, and no one seems to notice or even care. Many women suffer from acute feelings of low self-esteem. They have suffered so much that they have lost touch with who they really are. Their precarious situations have disempowered and disfigured them so much that they no longer know who they are. They feel inadequate and not good enough. Society has labelled them as "weaker vessels" and frantically attempted to prove the point. Consequently, these victims have become slaves to their silent fears and beliefs of inadequacy. They are tired of trying to no avail and have thrown in the towel. They have accepted their ill state as their fate. They have come to believe that what they are in the present is who they truly are. That's a lie!

This is what the devil wants you to believe. That's why he comes so hard at you with the diverse trials and temptations that befall you (1 Peter 5:8). They are all aimed at corroding your value and self-worth, at making you believe less of your true self so that you ultimately relinquish fulfilling your beautiful purpose in God. But he has failed already, because through the revelation of God's word and the eventual appreciation of your immense worth in Christ you will rise above the muddy waters of your past, look the devil straight in the face and spit into his eyes. You will trash your past and all the hurt that have held you down for so long, because now you *know* that you are the King's daughter and you are immeasurably loved!

Greater love has no one than this, than to lay down one's life for his friends.
– John 15:13

But God demonstrates His own love toward us, in that while we were still
sinners,
Christ died for us.
– Romans 5:8

For we do not have a High Priest who cannot sympathize with our weaknesses,
but was in all points tempted as we are, yet without sin.
– Hebrews 4:15

Nothing liberates from the shackles of low self-esteem and internal insecurity like knowing for sure that God is *your* Father and that He loves you very much. When I realized that Jesus knew exactly how I felt in my state of pain, I started my journey to healing and restoration, because then I realized that I could be open and vulnerable to Him and He would perfectly understand. He had walked the earth. He suffered rejection, loss, neglect, and betrayal too; so much that when He hung on the cross, He questioned the Father's love for Him. He was in pain (like I was, and you are) and couldn't feel the presence of His Father with Him, and He cried out. Thus, He is a been-there-done-that kind of Father. He perfectly understands and still loves us regardless.

No matter how ashamed of your past or present you may feel, know that that is the devil trying to steal away your confidence to weaken your capacity for excellent living; but you must refuse to yield. You are more than he's trying to make you believe about yourself. You are the daughter of the Most High God. You are a recipient of Jesus' life and love because Jesus has made you worthy and good enough. You are worthy of being loved and capable of giving love to others. You are all glorious within and without and filled with the very life of Christ with ability to do all things.

Woman, you *must* come to your senses; to the knowledge of who you are in Christ Jesus. This is what God is calling you to do right now through these pages. You are not a wimp! You were born with and for greatness. God is *your* Father, and He has a special soft spot for you. He cares very deeply for you, so much that He equated your value to the life of His only begotten son.

Where It Starts

Coming to a solemn realization of who you are in Christ is a journey, a process. It is not a sprint or dash, but more akin to a marathon. It is a journey that starts with the knowledge of the truth. Jesus said we shall know the truth and it shall *make* us free (John 8:32). The truth of God's

word is what liberates and makes free. Notice that Jesus was careful to use the word 'make' in that verse to communicate to us that a process is involved.

The truth you don't know or have a full grasp of is your greatest undoing. But I trust God that, as it pertains to your identity in Christ, this book will flood your spirit with liberating light!

They do not know, nor do they understand; they walk about in darkness;
all the foundations of the earth are unstable.
I said, "You are gods, and all of you are children of the Most High.
– Psalm 82:5-6

The only reason why God's people walk about in darkness, pain and frustration, and the foundations of our lives are unstable is simply because we don't know and understand God's truth concerning us. We are blind to the truth of God's word about our identity in Christ. And here's how that happens:

Whose minds the god of this age has blinded, who do not believe, lest the light
of the gospel of the glory of Christ, who is the image of God, should shine on
them.
– II Corinthians 4:4

The god of this age, the devil, blinds the minds of people against receiving the truth of God's word about them – the gospel, which is the power of God unto salvation, or liberty (Romans 1:16). And without knowledge of God's word, there cannot be faith, which, put otherwise, is acceptance. Understanding of God's word about you gives birth to faith in your heart, which empowers you to receive and walk in the reality that the word conveys.

Therefore, following knowledge of who you are in Christ is your total acceptance of this new reality that has been revealed to you. In other words, you must accept by faith who you now are in Christ; who the word says you are.

and receive with meekness the implanted word, which is able to save your souls. But be doers of the word, and not hearers only, deceiving yourselves.
– James 1:21b-22

God's word is only able to save your soul – liberate you – when you receive (accept) it with meekness as your new reality based on what is revealed in you. That is faith, without which it is impossible to please God (Hebrews 11:6). You must be a doer of the word.

I implore you, as you learn of your identity in the pages ahead, receive them with an open mind and accept them as your actual reality based on what Jesus accomplished for us in His death, burial and resurrection. This will ensure that the lessons are not only learned as head knowledge but are engrained into your spirit and practically manifest in your life. Let what you learn in the pages ahead mix with faith in your heart so it may profit you through and through. That will be my greatest joy – to see you free from the pain and shackles of your past and living in the full reality of your new identity in Christ.

Furthermore, peradventure you have been living in denial of your past hurts and ill experiences, you will need to undo that as you read on. Yes, I know it hurt so bad that you figured the best way to deal with it was to bottle it up and toss it away somewhere at the back of your mind. Well, I'm sorry to inform you that that didn't take away your pain; it only suppressed and concealed it temporarily. But a permanent solution is here now. He is the Balm in Gilead. So, I want you to dig it up and out in the open before the Lord. Tell him how much it hurts. Cry if you feel like; it's fine. The Lord understands. Just be totally open and vulnerable to Him. Any wound that is closed up without treatment may never heal. And, with this book in your hand and by the power of the Holy Spirit, the Lord wants to heal you permanently from that pain and hurt. Open it up to Him, hand it over to Him and let go. Let Him do what He does better than anyone else – healing hurts and pain.

Therefore, humble yourselves under the mighty hand of God, that He may exalt you in due time, casting all your care upon Him, for He cares for you.
– I Peter 5:6-7

The Lord cares deeply for you and He can be totally trusted. Cast that pain upon Him now. He loves you unrepentantly!

Abide in His Love

As the Father loved Me, I also have loved you; abide in My love.
– John 15:9

For He Himself has said, "I will never leave you nor forsake you." So, we may boldly say: "The Lord is my helper; I will not fear. What can man do to me?"
– Hebrews 13:5-6

The scriptures above are instructions for continually living in the consciousness of God's love for us. First, you must be filled and satisfied with the knowledge of God's love for you, and from that depth of assurance, expel fear from your heart. Then, you must draw closer to God by developing your love relationship with Him through faith in your heart and on your lips, confessing your knowledge of His love for you.

Knowing who you are and whom you carry on your inside makes you stand out and stand tall. We love Him because He first loved us by going all the way to die for us and redeem us back to God, giving us eternal life. Whoever acknowledges that Jesus is the Son of God has God living in him and he is in God, because he has known and believed the love that God has for us (I John 4:15-16). Learn to live with this beautiful consciousness every day through meditation on the word.

No Fear in Love

There is no fear in love; but perfect love casts out fear, because fear involves torment. But he who fears has not been made perfect in love.
– I John 4:18

Please read that verse of scripture again. You see, one of the devil's greatest weapons against us is fear – the fear that we are not worthy or that we are not good enough; the fear of failure, rejection, repression, criticism, etc. The devil uses autosuggestion, mostly based on what we have experienced in the past, to hold us down with fear. He suggests disempowering thoughts to our minds, and we cringe, especially when he reminds us of an experience that serves as a point of reference. For example, if you were raped in the past, the devil continually tells you that you are defiled and filthy and so are not good enough to enjoy the things you desire or that God says are yours. If you were physically molested as a child, he keeps the memory fresh in your mind and tells you that you are unwanted and ugly. He cripples you with the fear of rejection and not being good enough. If you have experienced a string of failures or perpetual lack before, he tries to convince you that you can never succeed because you're a no-good. Even worse, he muffles your voice and keeps you from speaking out, even to seek help.

Oh, I feel like screaming at the top of my voice right now to tell you: DAUGHTER OF GOD, THAT DEVIL HAS BEEN *LYING* TO YOU! *ENOUGH!* Enough of believing the devil's lame and baseless lies! I ask you, *whose report will you believe: The Lord who loves you infinitely and has proven it or the devil who has contributed no stake whatsoever to your life other than to destroy it?* Who will you believe? Fear has torment, and it is the devil's favourite weapon for crippling God's people. But are you not tired of living in fear as a shadow of your true self? Salvation is here, child of God. Embrace it. It is God's undiluted, unadulterated love.

God's perfect love casts out and banishes the devil's fears from your life permanently. He who fears has not been made perfect in love. That means, if you find that your fears are still reigning over you, then you are yet to come to full understanding of God's undying, unflinching love for you – the very love that nailed Jesus to the cross, sent Him to the grave, and resurrected Him on the third day to give you and I direct access to the Father. It is the same love that gave us the Spirit of Adoption by whom we can now call God, Father. Oh, how that sentence stirred up sweet bubbles in my tummy as I wrote it! Sweet love of a sweet Father!

Perfect love casts out fear. So, yes, the devil is right that you were not good enough to enjoy anything from God. But you were not the only one who wasn't good enough. It was all of us – every human being. At best, our righteousness is as filthy rag before God. That is exactly why Jesus came as our substitute to bear the penalty for our sin and to qualify us for righteousness – right standing with God. And, after those three days and two nights in the belly of the earth, your debts were *fully* and *eternally* paid off, dear daughter of Zion. Right now, *you are qualified* and *good enough* through Jesus Christ. You have been *accepted in the Beloved* (Ephesians 1:6). Once you received Jesus into your heart, His righteousness was imputed unto you and you instantly became a child of God, fully qualified for every good thing that is available in God. This is such a beautiful and wholesome mystery, some of which we will explore as we proceed.

But first, right now I want you to look straight ahead with a defiant face, stemming from this new realization, and tell the devil to *get lost*, with all his fears and lies, because the perfect love of Jesus has set you free and qualified you! Hallelujah! Satan no longer has any legal hold on your life if you are in Christ, unless you allow him through ignorance.

For God has not given us a spirit of fear, but of power and of love and of a sound mind.
– II Timothy 1:7

Now, let us examine your identity as the King's daughter as outlined in different portions of His word to us.

Who you are in Christ
1.   You are Redeemed
Christ has redeemed us from the curse of the law, having become a curse for us (for it is written, "Cursed is everyone who hangs on a tree", that the blessing of Abraham might come on the Gentiles in Christ Jesus, that we might receive the promise of the Spirit through faith.
– Galatians 3:13-14

One thing you must settle in your heart is that you are *not* cursed. In this part of the world, often when people are faced with unfortunate circumstances, their default conclusion is that they must be cursed. Well, that may be true for anyone who is outside of Christ but not for the woman who is now in Christ. No, you are blessed forever. You *cannot* be cursed. Generational curses do not run in your family (the bloodline of Jesus). Only permanent blessings flow in that family. So, toss out that lie of the devil from your mind; you are not cursed, but blessed and favoured. All the devil wants, is to make you believe otherwise so that you don't enjoy the full potential of what God has in store for you. You are blessed! Redeemed unto God!

2.   *You are Perfect*

*And every priest stands ministering daily and offering repeatedly
the same sacrifices, which can never take away sins.
But this Man, after He had offered one sacrifice for sins forever,
sat down at the right hand of God,
from that time waiting till His enemies are made His footstool.
For by one offering He has PERFECTED FOREVER those who are
being sanctified.* – Hebrews 10:11-14

As women, we care about too many unnecessary things: what people
think of you, how you look, what people are saying behind your back,
your figure, your nails, your hair, your lashes, etc. Is it wrong to care
about these? Not necessarily, but not at the expense of your true worth.
You cannot allow these mundane things to be the determinants of your
self-worth and sense of value. That is an aberration. Remember what
Jesus said to Martha when she complained that her sister, Mary would
not help her in the kitchen? He said, *Martha, Martha, you are worried and
troubled about many things. But one thing is needed* (Luke 10:41b-42a). What
is the one thing that is needed? What God says about you! That's all,
nothing else matters. No one else's opinion is needed. God says you are
perfect, complete and whole in Christ. Believe that and it's settled.

3.   *You are Righteous*

*Therefore, if anyone is in Christ, he is a new creation; old things are passed
away; behold, all things have become new.
For He made Him who knew no sin to be sin for us, that we
might become the righteousness of God in Him.*
– II Corinthians 5:17,21

The only question to ask yourself here is: Am I in Christ? If your answer
is yes, then you *are* righteous. It does not matter what the world has told
you before now, or how many sins you committed in the past, or even

the weight of your sins. God doesn't care. The minute you received Jesus into your life, you became a brand-new being. God literally forgot that you ever committed any sin. In fact, as far as God is concerned, you have *never* sinned!

Yes, I know. That sounds preposterous and blasphemous, right? Well, I didn't say it; God Himself did: *I, even I, am He who blots out your transgressions for My own sake; and I will not remember your sins* (Isaiah 43:25). God has forgotten your sins; it's time to forget them too. Righteousness is the nature of God that we put on at the instance of salvation. You don't do right to be righteous; you *receive* righteousness and become righteous. Consequently, you do and live right *because* you are righteous by being a partaker of His divine nature.

4.   *You are Precious*

For God so loved the world that He gave His ONLY begotten Son .
– John 3:16
For you were bought at a price
– I Corinthians 6:20

Most women have different kinds of jewelleries, some made of different precious stones. You will agree with me that just as their values in the market differ, so also is the value we place on each of them. A 24karat gold earring cannot be kept in the same place and manner a gold-platted earring is kept. The difference is in their worth and value to us. In like manner, you are more precious to God than all the precious stones in the world put together. In fact, you are worth the life of Jesus to Him, which is why He willingly sacrificed Jesus so that He could have you as His daughter. Then He gave you a seat right beside Him in all His splendour and glory. *And raised us up together, and made us sit together in the heavenly places in Christ Jesus* (Ephesians 2:6).

5.   *You have an Inheritance*

The Spirit Himself bears witness with our spirit that we are children of God, and if children, then heirs—heirs of God and joint heirs with Christ, if indeed we suffer with Him, that we may also be glorified together.
– Romans 8:16-17

Giving thanks to the Father, who has qualified us to share in the inheritance of the saints in light.
– Colossians 1:12

Blessed be the God and Father of our Lord Jesus Christ, who has blessed us with every spiritual blessing in the heavenly places in Christ.
– Ephesians 1:3

An heir is anyone who legally qualifies for an inheritance. That means that as a joint-heir with Jesus, who is our eldest brother in God's kingdom (Colossians1:15-18), we qualify to inherit all that God owns. I am thrilled by this truth even as I write it. God is our Father and He has qualified us through Jesus to inherit all that are His. Therefore, we have no business being small and struggling through life. We have no business with sickness, poverty, pain, and rejection, because our Father has given us the victory already. We only need to appropriate the victory that is ours every time these ugly circumstances rear up.

6.   *You have the Spirit of Wisdom and Revelation*

But you have an anointing from the Holy One, and you know all things.
– I John 2:20
For as many as are led by the Spirit of God, these are the [daughters] *of God.*
– Romans 8:14 (emphasis mine)

The sensitivity of the Holy Spirit is resident and active inside you. You perceive things that you can't explain. You know when to act and when not to, if only you learn to yield to the leading of the Holy Spirit inside you. You are a daughter of God because His Spirit leads you and keeps you from harm while ordering your steps to the place of prosperity and peace. He teaches your heart what to do per time and in every given situation. His peace is the umpire of your heart, leading you to right decisions for yourself and others within your sphere of influence. Beyond your head, you know things through your heart. And the more you yield to the Holy Spirit, the more He teaches and guides you into greatness.

7.   *You are a Life Giver*

And so, it is written, "The first man Adam became a living being." The last Adam became a life-giving spirit.
– I Corinthians 15:45

You are a life-giving spirit in the order of Jesus, the last Adam. Because you have His life inside you, you have been empowered to extend the power of that life to the world around you. Apostle Paul advised the Corinthian church to follow him as he followed Christ. That means he was modelling Christ's life to them. In like manner, God has empowered you to model His life to your children and other people around you. He picked you up from the miry clay, cleansed you and equipped you to be a representation of His life to the world. You are a light through whom other people should be lit up. You are an example of godly and impactful living. People should look at you to learn how to respond to life's situations, how to recover and walk in self-confidence in Christ. This is your ministry in Christ.

You are a reservoir of kindness and warmth; despite whatever challenges you may have confronted in your past. In Christ, your past has been wiped away forever and you now have the heart of kindness and warmth of your Father. You have allowed the Holy Spirit to heal your wounds from the past and empower you with capacity to love and to care deeply for those around you.

Hold on to Your Confidence

And do not be conformed to this world, but be transformed by the renewing of your mind, that you may prove what is that good and acceptable and perfect will of God.
– Romans 12:2

Therefore, do not cast away your confidence, which has great reward But we are not of those who draw back to perdition, but of those who believe to the saving of the soul.
– Hebrews 10:35,39

If you lose your confidence in these truths of God's word about you, then you will always be a victim to life's whims and the cruelty of our world. Rather, meditate on them every day until they become deep-seated in your soul and become your daily reality. Your confidence in God's word has great reward; guard it jealously.

Therefore, since we have such a hope, we are very bold.
– 2 Corinthians 3:12

Realities of the King's Daughter

- The King's daughter is all glorious within. *(Psalms 4:7)*
- You are a member of God's own royal family, a recipient of Jesus Christ's life and love.
- Through your faith in Jesus Christ as Lord and Saviour, you have been adopted by God and given a whole new identity in Christ.
- As the King's daughter, you are of God's royal family, highly cherished and given access to the fullness of His love and provision. You are *not* a slave or a hired hand for God.
- You are a cherished daughter, an heir of God. *(Romans 8:16-17)*
- Everything belonging to Jesus is yours by relationship. All that He is, you are. *(I John 4:17)*

- You are filled with the very life of Christ to do all things. (*Philippians 4:13*)
- You are a new creation endued with the very life of Jesus Christ. (*I Corinthians 5:17*)
- There is no condemnation for you in Christ. (*Romans 8:1*)
- You house the very life of Jesus and the very same power that raised Him from the dead. (*Romans 8:11*)
- You are no longer a slave to fear and you have the Spirit of Adoption. (*II Timothy 1:7, Romans 8:15*)
- You are an heir of God and joint heir with Christ Jesus. (*Romans 8:17*)
- You are created to walk in glorious liberty and the world is waiting for the manifestation of Christ through you to the nations. (*Romans 8:19*)
- You are royalty. We've been made kings and priests unto our God. (*Revelations 5:10*)
- You are bold, audacious and daring. The righteous is bold as a lion. (*Proverbs 28:1*)
- You are endowed with the strength of Christ. (*Philippians 4:13*)
- You are confident.

These and many more are who you are in Christ, and you must embrace it and walk in the reality thereof.

Chapter

THREE

HER STRUGGLES

Is there a chance that all you went through (or are going through) was for a purpose and worked behind the scenes to bring you to where you are now? Is it possible that those experiences were a bridge to bring you to the vantage point where you stand right now? Were you being pruned for a giant task in the future? I believe you were. I was too. Every experience, whether good or bad, was allowed for a reason. Now, I know that this is quite tricky, so let me clarify.

The Bible says that God cannot be tempted with evil and He does not tempt any man. That means God cannot orchestrate or support evil. However, because we live in an imperfect world that is governed by imperfect men, most of whom yield to the devil's influence, you will be tempted with evil. It is the devil's way of attempting to break you so hard that you will not be able to accomplish God's plans for your life, or even consider them.

Through the ages, Satan has noticed that God's strategy for bringing solutions into the world is through new babies. He knows from experience that every child born on earth carries a solution for an aspect of life's problems. And as they grow, a time comes when God empowers them to deliver their solutions. Therefore, in an attempt to thwart God's purposes, he launches different kinds of attacks on every child through to adulthood. Yet, what his foolishness blinds his eyes to is the fact that God *always* turns around all the devil's works to favour His sons and daughters. That's why the Bible says, "*And we know that all things work together for good to those who love God, to those who are called according to His purpose*" (Romans 8:28).

1 Corinthians 10:13, AMP, also says, *No temptation [regardless of its source] has overtaken or enticed you that is not common to human experience [nor is any temptation unusual or beyond human resistance]; but God is faithful [to His word – He is compassionate and trustworthy], and He will not let you be tempted beyond your ability [to resist], but along with the temptation He [has in the past and is now and] will [always] provide the way out as well, so that you will be able to endure it [without yielding, and will overcome temptation with joy].*

What the devil does for evil, God turns to work good for you. He strengthens you in it so that it makes you rather than break you. In your weak times, He avails you His strength to carry you through.

Haven't you ever wondered how you survived those times unbroken? Haven't you wondered how, though you were deeply pained, you somehow found strength to continue living and to hope for better days? That was God, your loving Father. He was right there with you all along, holding your hand and going through the high waters and deep valleys with you. Yes, you couldn't see Him, and it didn't feel as though He heard your many screams, but He was right there strengthening and cheering you on to keep going. There is greater joy lying in wait for you in the future. You needed to become a *certain kind of person*; the kind who could undertake and execute the task ahead. It was all part of a master plan. And the devil was a pawn in God's hand, executing God's purposes while in self-deceit of succeeding at destroying God's agenda for your life. He failed with Jesus and has failed with you too. He thought that suffering and killing Jesus was victory for him, yet that exact act was his eternal defeat. Hallelujah!

Likewise, what the enemy meant for evil when he caused me to suffer so much pain, God turned it for good and today He is using my story and victory to heal many women who have been hurt in the past. All glory to His name! And He will do it with yours, too. I will share a few.

A Girl Starved of Love

I was betrayed by nearly everyone I knew growing up: uncles, aunts, cousins, friends, domestic helps, etc. I was pretty much a happy child until I turned 6. My father had died 2 years earlier and my mum sent me to live with my father's brother in Lagos, leaving her behind with my siblings. My uncle was a high-ranking military officer at the time and travelled a lot.

At the time I joined him, he was still married but had no child with his wife. She had her younger sister, who was about my age living with them and we got along well like sisters.

My Uncle's wife took care of me like her own daughter and gave me all I needed. She introduced me to reading books and ensured I ate well. She was very much a lovely woman. However, barely two years of living with them, their marriage hit the rocks and she moved out with her sister. With that, my life went sour.

With my uncle always either out of Lagos or Nigeria altogether, I was left at the mercy of the domestic staff in the house. And, being a child and naïve, I was unassuming and wanted to please everyone around me. I sought attention by trying to be a good child who was respectful and courteous, but it seemed as though the more I tried, the less I was liked. Maybe if my uncle had been very fond of me, the dislike I got from my many adult-housemates would have been justified, given that they might have thought of me as a spoiled, privileged child. But no, my uncle was a typical military man who would come home late almost every night (when he was in town), sit by the TV set while sipping one of his assorted alcoholic drinks from a glass, then leave later for his room upstairs. I craved for his love and attention but never got any. I would fix his room, collect his bag from the car sometimes, serve him whatever he needed, but no warmth came from him. So, I was left to myself and alone. And my predators took advantage of the situation, knowing that I had no recourse in my uncle. I was framed for stealing money from his purse, starved of food and provisions when I went to school, and even one time I was left alone for three days in my room when I fell ill. They dismissed my claim and concluded that I was lazy and didn't want to work. I was left in my room with a high fever and no proper food. Thank God for an aunt who visited and asked after me, only to find me almost lifeless in my room. I was rushed to the hospital and was immediately treated for an emergency case. I still remember the nurses running helter-skelter to quickly lower my temperature and keep it from tipping off. I was wheeled into the ward and admitted with acute malaria fever.

You know, it is often easier to bear the pains of whatever torturous situations you might be faced with when you know that you committed some offence to warrant the pain. But when you search your heart for what you did wrong to merit such affliction and can't find any, it could be most devastating. It is even worse when you're only 8 years old. I yearned for a little show of love and affection, but no one cared to blink an eye. I was starved and deprived of the one thing I longed for the most – some love.

In my junior secondary school, I would write and submit my list of school items to my uncle and he will issue out money for the items to be gotten for me. However, I only ever got my full provision any time my uncle was at home when I was to go back to school; but God help me whenever he wasn't home!

I remember this time when I submitted my list as usual and continued reminding the adult in charge as my resumption day approached. After much reluctance, one morning she asked me to get dressed for the market. Finally! I thought. So, I excitedly got ready. We got to the market, entered a grocery store and she asked me to get the things I needed. Happily, I picked as much as I needed off the shelves. When I was done, she asked me to pay! Shocked to the bone, I stood looking at her and wondering what she meant by that. When I saw that she meant business, I carefully selected the items the 500 naira I brought along with me, which I'd gathered from cash gifts, could afford. I paid and we left the market. That was all I resumed school with. Besides all these, they always promised to visit me on visiting days but never came, until I grew used to not being visited like other kids in school (I was a boarding student). This further reinforced my feeling of not being loved or wanted.

A Thief Who Never Stole a Thing

I had an aunt who lived in Lagos too at the time. One day she came visiting when my uncle was home. Typical of me, I was happy to see her, so I lurked around in the living room as they conversed. But before long, my uncle made a comment I couldn't believe. He called me a thief, telling my aunt that I had a habit of stealing money from his purse. That pierced my heart very deeply. But what was worse was that neither of them thought to give me room to explain. I was in rude shock and lost for how to respond.

I thought hard and long about that accusation, trying to understand why my uncle would think I stole his money. The only explanation that came to my mind was that I must have been deliberately framed by one of the adult housemates. Countless times, I had been given my uncle's purse by one staff or another to take to him, mostly on mornings after he had left it in the living room the previous night. Apparently, someone used to take out money from the purse and then hand the empty purse to the unassuming and naïve Becky to take to her uncle, who in turn concluded that the 8-year-old girl who brought his purse to him was the thief. How convenient for him! There was never even a question to clarify who did.

With no one to discuss my plight with, I would only cry every time I remembered the accusation. And that made me lose hope of ever winning my uncle's affection, so I quit trying. Life was forcing me to grow up fast.

Why me? I asked myself for many days. Why does Daddy (as I called him) hate me so much? Can the world just end already? I wanted to die. No answers came. I began to lose my voice and confidence. I became a loner and an introvert especially because I still had other struggles.

Another incident comes to mind; this time much more devastating because I was already a young adult and the accusation happened in front of several people but in my absence. It was at a relative's wedding. I was in the university at the time and had to leave school amidst meagre resources and much inconvenience to travel to this wedding. At the time, I didn't like attending weddings but had to attend this one because of how I esteemed this relative. So, I embarked on the trip with joy.

On the morning of the wedding, all the bride's maids, friends, sisters and relatives were all in their assigned bedroom together with the bride when suddenly one lady exclaimed that her pair of earrings for the wedding ceremony was missing. Surprised and irritated, we all immediately started to search the room for them. Soon we found one of the pair, yet the lady wouldn't stop lamenting loudly for the other one. Well, in my mind, I was wondering why the continued outcry and loud noise; since one had been found, it simply meant the other would be found too. But the ladies just kept yelling about how it was an expensive earring. I started to get irritated. And when I couldn't stand the noise anymore, in my typical manner at the time, I quietly walked out of the room for them to continue searching.

Suddenly there was an outburst that it had been found and I heard it from the living room where I was. I went in almost immediately, and said, "I told you it will be found." No one answered me, as they continued to dress up for the occasion. Nothing suggested the need to ask where they found it since the ladies didn't put up any suspicious attitude, or maybe I was too unsuspecting to notice.

We went for the wedding, finished and returned home later by evening, only for one of my aunts to tell me that the earring was found in my travelling bag. I told her that wasn't possible. First, because I didn't take them, and second, my bag was zipped and locked with a key, which I had with me when I left the room. Then she said it was found in the side pockets. That wasn't all; she also said she was told that I was caught the previous night trying to unbuckle a cousin's bangle in the middle of the night. Oh my!

This broke me and I started to tear up so uncontrollably than I'd ever done before, especially because I had been labelled a thief since morning and no one told me, so that I could at least, try to clear my name. I only got to know after the wedding was over and most of the ladies had travelled back to their base. No wonder the side talks and murmurings every time I passed by people sitting in clusters throughout that day, I thought. I felt so terrible and deeply regretted travelling to that wedding in the first place.

My molestation experiences!

Yes, I was sexually molested in those early years too, and only narrowly escaped rape severally. I still remember each experience as though they happened yesterday. When I was about seven years old, I had just showered, only to realize that I needed to pick up my nightdress from the laundry room. So, I headed downstairs to get it.

When I got in, the laundry guy was there and asked what I came for and I told him. He reached for it, held it out to me and told me to come over and collect it. As I reached him to collect my nightdress he quickly pulled me close, removed my towel, pushed me to the floor and started to press on my bare chest and was attempting to make his way to my lower parts when, thankfully, we heard footsteps of someone approaching the laundry and he quickly stopped and left me to see who it was. That was my saving grace because I got the chance to leave, befuddled at what happened and what his intentions were. My parents were not around, so I couldn't tell anyone what happened; I kept it to myself.

Several other attempts were made at different times, but the first experience had given me a clue to what they wanted, so I was ready. I thought of how to escape and what to look out for subsequently. I was careful to avoid being alone with any of the domestic workers.

Interestingly, there were incidents that seemed as though there was a unanimous conspiracy to get one of them to have his way with me. One, that shook me and that would change my entire outlook on life was when my father travelled, and all the staff came into the sitting room to watch a TV program. One minute, we were all together and the next minute, everyone started to leave, including the female folks. I was initially oblivious to what was going on because I was so engrossed with the screen. Before I realized it, one of the male staff came over to where I sat and attempted to pull me unto himself. You can't imagine the horror of having a grown man trying to force himself on an eight years old child. I cried and shouted, begging for release to no avail. Then I got a break and ran towards the two doors, one after the other, and to my greatest dismay, both were locked. So, I continued shouting ever so loudly and running from end to end of the room. However, what I didn't understand, till date, was why no one came to help despite the loud shouts for help and the bangs on the doors.

After a sustained period of fighting and resisting he gave up and finally released me.

My life took a different turn from that moment. I started living in fear of everyone. I didn't know what to expect any more. I couldn't bring myself to trust anyone from that day. Everyone, to me, was a potential assailant.

A predator who was forthright with his attempts was an ADC to my uncle. He was a man of big stature. In my uncle's absence, he ruled the house, being the highest-ranking staff in the house. Maybe that was why he felt bold to fondle my tender body whenever he wished. He would call me to sit on his thigh outside the house and in his office, and he would fondle my body. Of course, I hated what he did, but I was too afraid to speak out. Besides, who was I going to tell when it would be my words against his? Plus, every other staff in the house feared him as well. The only person I could have told was my uncle had no faith in whatever I had to say.

I remember that dealing with that officer was the first prayer point I had when I got born again at age 11, just after I resumed secondary school. I made some new friends who were born again and active in fellowship, and they led me to Christ and introduced me to a senior student who took it upon himself to teach me scriptures. As soon as I learned to pray and expect God to answer, my prayer point was for God to get rid of that man for me. And my loving Father answered me. I always dreaded going home because of him. But at the end of this particular term, when I got home, I learned that my uncle's ADC had been changed and replaced with not just anybody, but a God-fearing Deeper Life Bible Church member – one who always ensured I attended fellowship in school and prayed and studied my Bible when on holiday. That was liberation for me. Glory! You can't even imagine my excitement.

When You Start to Blame Yourself

You can't imagine the effect of these episodes on my psyche. I practically lived in fear of every grown man. I struggled with hurts and pains for years causing me to limit myself in so many ways. When something happens once, it can easily pass as happenstance. But when it repeats itself more times than you can count and is orchestrated by different people, it becomes a pattern. Your mind begins to wonder why. You ask over and over until only one answer reverberates in your mind: *you are to blame.* However, you are never able to say how exactly you caused the predicament. You just conclude that you must have done something wrong to deserve the horror. Maybe you offended

God somehow and He decided to punish you this way. That was my naive conclusion.

Aside being labelled a thief by the man who was supposed to be my father and being assaulted several times, I was maltreated in more ways than I can count by different people. There was the driver who suddenly began failing to come get me after school hours as instructed by the caretaker at that time. I learned to leave school and walk home on the streets of Lagos once it was 5.00 PM and no one had come for me. This further reinforced what I had already come to accept in my mind – no one cared for me.

The maltreatments continued into university. My uncle always gave me meagre amounts of money to take to school, and that left me almost perpetually broke every semester. What was worse was having the label of being the daughter of a renowned retired military officer in town and yet struggling financially. I simply had to toss out the label from my mind and face my reality and concern myself with how to get by every day. Thank God for great friends and fellowship that provided strength to hold on and keep going. Also, there were yet other incidences that revived the label of being a thief during this time. But pained as I felt, I still found inner strength to keep holding on.

It was during this period that I met a friend who became my sister from another mother, and her wonderful family became the family I never really had. I will not complete this book without telling of what a blessing she was to me during this phase of my life.

You see, my situation was so bad that, literally, there were days I did not have clothes or shoes to wear for lectures, days I had to live on the mercy of roommates for food to eat, soap to bath with, toothpaste to brush my teeth, slippers, shoes, and clothes to wear. This would go on for weeks and months sometimes. In fact, in my fourth year of schooling, I couldn't afford to pay for my accommodation because my uncle didn't give me school fees at all that year. My friends contributed to pay my school fees for me. And as you might imagine, that year was very challenging for me. I slept anywhere I was given permission to sleep, until this precious friend offered I stay in her room, she finally rescued me. It was apparently not convenient for her and her roommates, but she sacrificed all the same. Oh, God bless her for me! She was an angel sent to me at that period.

Her family also played a significant role in my life: housing me, feeding me, and meeting some basic needs when I was on break; since I had decided to break free from being dependent on my uncle after that act of refusing to pay my tuition for that year. This family gave me my first idea of an ideal home, which I had never experienced. Her parents were so loving and caring, and so were all her siblings. I can never forget them! She became a sister to me – so caring and sacrificial. Indeed, the Bible is so correct when it says, "There is a friend that sticks closer than a brother" (Proverbs 18:24).

This connects me back to the question that opened this chapter: Is there a chance that all you went through (or are going through) was for a purpose and worked behind the scenes to bring you to where you are now? You see, yes, I had a broken childhood, and not because of anything I did wrong, but because Satan was trying to frustrate God's purposes for my life while God was busy using the very stones he was throwing at me to build my life onto the peak of my calling in Christ. Here I am today: I don't look like what I have been through. My life in the present is a total detachment from the person I was while growing up. Life beat me so hard and left me very broken, lacking confidence and belief in myself. But my darling King-Father gathered the broken pieces and recreated a whole and complete woman – the Becky you know or are reading about today. Oh, I just can't thank Him enough!

A SIDE STORY:
The Reason everything won't be Perfect

I run a beauty salon. One day, shortly after we started, a young lady came in to make her hair. As is my manner, I exchanged pleasantries with her but quickly noticed that she was in pain, so I was moved to hold a conversation with her. Thankfully she was open to talk about it. She told me she had an appointment with her doctor later that day because she was having a threatened abortion. Moved with compassion, I immediately said a prayer for her to the effect that she will not lose the pregnancy in Jesus name. But to my dismay, instead of saying amen to the prayer, she said, "No, no, no, no. Jesus has nothing to do with my pregnancy. The final state of my pregnancy would be the result of the expertise of the doctors, not Jesus." Those words swept me off my feet faster than a tornado would! Am I face-to-face with an atheist? I asked myself. I certainly didn't see that coming. My lady-customer continued, "Jesus does not exist. Even God doesn't exist. They are only superheroes made up by men." Then she dropped the bomb, "I don't even believe there is a hell. And in case there is, I don't mind going there!" Oh my! I muttered. Were my ears hearing correctly or was I dreaming on my feet?

I started to use every scripture I knew that could change this lady's heart, but to no avail. Then I realized an even sadder fact – she was once a devoted Christian. She knew all the scriptures I quoted. Her argument was this: if God is Almighty, why is there evil in the world? Why do we attribute good to God and when things are bad, we say it's the devil? Why are people dying from hunger, sicknesses and terrorism and God is doing nothing about it? It is so because he doesn't really exist, because if he does, he should have done something; he won't watch people die.

It became pointless trying to convince her against her belief once I realized that she was once a believer. I simply said to her, "God will reveal Himself to you in a way that you will be *so* sure of Him." Apparently, she must have gone through a lot of heartaches and perhaps seeing loved ones die through sickness, among other things. She couldn't stand through the tests of life. She missed the mark and derailed.

This encounter was an eye-opener for me to realize that there is still plenty work to be done for Christ on earth. How can the Church get people saved through one door and lose other people through another? It reminded me of the scripture in Matthew 7:24-27. The storm will surely come down, the waters will surely rise, and the winds will surely beat against every house, but only the house that is firmly grounded upon the rock, which is Christ, can stand victorious. We know that Christ is the Word. How many Christians are rooted and grounded in the word today? I am not talking about head knowledge, but revelation knowledge of Christ.

> *That he would grant you, according to the riches of his glory, to be strengthened with might by his Spirit in the inner man;*
>
> *That Christ may dwell in your hearts by faith; that ye, being rooted and grounded in love,*
>
> *May be able to comprehend with all saints what is the breadth, and length, and depth, and height;*

And to know the love of Christ, which passeth knowledge, that ye might be filled with all the fulness of God.

– Ephesians 3:16-19, KJV

The hearts of men need to be flooded with the light of God's word so that they can be deeply rooted and grounded to withstand tests and trials. Our responsibility as children of God is to ensure that men and women are fed properly and discipled into the fullness of Christ, in season and out of season. This is expedient because times of trials and tribulations will surely come, when each person's faith will be tried.

I told myself that I am not doing enough as a daughter of the Most High. Men should not see us and question the existence of God. If that is happening, it is because we have failed to rise to the occasion of our purpose, identity, knowledge of our capabilities and manifesting same to our world. They that know their God will be strong and do exploits (Daniel 11:32). Manifestations are not meant for the church, but for the world. We are not meant to sit in our buildings having diverse manifestations of the Spirit, but to take them out there to people who have lost hope and trust in the love and divinity of our God.

This is a call to awake to duty. Let's take who we are, our responsibilities as sons and daughters more seriously. One reason the church is not manifesting is because we have refused to grow. We have chosen to remain in the baby-stage of Christianity, not wanting to mature. Only sons manifest, only sons take up responsibilities, only sons adhere to and execute instructions. Darkness covers the earth, and gross darkness blankets the people. Let's rise and shine like sons of God that we are so men can see us and glorify our Father in heaven.

Since we have received the grace of God, in our respective spheres of influence, we have the power to exert the authority we have in Christ to cut off the devil's influence. Sadly, not many of us know and exercise this power. Therefore, our world – even our own lives – remains in chaos. We have not learnt to appropriate the power of Jesus to our surrounding to cause God's will to *be done on earth as it is in heaven* (Matthew 6:10).

God does not act on earth without the cooperation of a man somewhere on earth. This is one reason why we pray – to enforce God's will on earth. And except believers intercept the devil's schemes per time, he will always have his way; especially when he can find men who are yielded to him to execute his will.

Like God requires a man to enforce and execute His will on earth per time, Satan also works through men. That is why every time you have been hurt in the past; you did not see the devil directly; it happened through a fellow human being. So, by extension, our world is in such deep chaos because there are men yielded to the enemy who is committed to wrecking as much havoc on mankind as possible before his time is up – and he knows it is short.

Nevertheless, the beauty of it all is that Jesus has given us victory and power to live above the wickedness of the enemy, regardless of how they manifest and through whom. You and I are the victorious ones in Christ. Therefore, it is an aberration and a waste of the sacrifice of Jesus for us to live as victims. That should not be heard of about us!

Does this mean you will not be confronted with challenges? You will. But face them from the depth of knowledge of who you are in Christ, knowing that you are victorious and a conqueror already, and never a victim. Let your knowledge of God and who He's made you guard your heart.

The Brutal Reality

In our world, women are vulnerable and exposed to so much harm. And mostly, this starts when we are children – very much vulnerable – and continues into adulthood. The world seems devoted to sapping out our power and unique strengths. The enemy knows that we are powerful and specially empowered by God to fill the world with greatness (Genesis 3:15b), and so he hates the woman and works hard to keep her trampled. But thanks be to God who always causes us to triumph in Christ Jesus.

Every day, society seeks to cripple the woman by hitting hard at her person. Women are victims of various attacks: from sexual assaults to domestic violence, trafficking, discrimination, lack of education, emotional hurts, corporate victimization, professional predation, etc. Women are constantly being hit and no one seems to care. Statistics abound and are worrisome. See an example below:

Findings from a National Survey carried out in 2014 on Violence Against Children in Nigeria confirmed that one in four females reported experiencing sexual violence in childhood with approximately 70% reporting more than one incident of sexual violence. In the same study, it was found that 24.8% of females of ages 18 to 24 years experienced sexual abuse prior to age 18, of which 5% sought help, with only 3.5% receiving any services.[1]

The big question begging for answer now is: to whom shall the downtrodden turn for help and rescue? There is only one who can truly and permanently save. His name is Jesus Christ. He is your King and Father; the one who loves you with an everlasting love and has vowed to save you to the uttermost. He already gave you His ultimate – His life. So, now that He lives and reigns over all, there is nothing He cannot give you or do for you. He is love personified and He abounds generously towards you. All you need do is ask for His help. Thankfully, He does not only bring you out, He also makes you a bundle of solutions to your world. After you are tried, you come forth as pure, refined gold, ready and equipped to add value to your world.

Struggles in life are common but are customized per person. According to Romans 8:15, the Spirit we received does not make us slaves to live in fear again, rather He brought about our adoption to daughterhood, and by Him we are able to call God 'Abba Father'. Hallelujah!

Knowing that we are sojourners in this world and not citizens should make us handle every situation differently – spiritually. That is what makes the difference. The situations we face come to test our identity and purpose. Situations don't determine who we are, rather we determine the effect they have on us. Fear, low self-esteem, guilt, and bitterness should not be found in us.

As the King's daughter, the only past you have is in Christ. He made you a brand ambassador of His kingdom. Therefore, don't allow yourself to be limited by the situations you were sent to dominate and influence for the kingdom. Live above them, because you are truly above them all. You are seated together with Christ at the right hand of God in heaven right this minute. We must come to our senses, have a mind renewal, and arise and do what the kingdom bids.

What if You were Mary?

Have you ever thought about the plight of Mary, the mother of Jesus; what she had to endure to see the accomplishment of God's prophecy to her through the angel Gabriel? Let us examine her life together.

Mary was a pretty, virgin damsel who lived at a time when chastity was the norm. Virginity was so highly esteemed that a man had the right to make it public knowledge if he found out after wedding that his bride was not a virgin. And that potentially got the woman stoned to death, according to Jewish custom. Yet, here was this young lady who was minding her business and patiently awaiting her memorable wedding day but one day got a visit that altered her life forever. An angel appeared to her and told her she would conceive by some supernatural means. Imagine her immediate dilemma for a bit.

With this phase passed, contrary to what Mary must have expected as a birthplace for her baby – since the angel said he would be the Saviour of the world, he was born in a manger and not a fancy hospital. What's the correlation between a manger and greatness? How could the Saviour of the *world* – not only Israel – be born in a manger? Even if all the fancy places in Bethlehem were fully booked, couldn't God have worked something out? Why is He God, after all? And He said this child is His Son? Or did the angel lie to her? Something seemed amiss with this construct. Again, I can only imagine the contemplations of Mary's heart. But she was a wise woman. She knew to trust the One who gave the word. It's His purpose after all, so let Him accomplish it however He deemed fit.

As if that was not enough to plague her mind, there came Herod seeking to kill the little baby, and all God saw fit to do was to ask them to escape with the child. Seriously! This certainly didn't sound like the God their fathers told them about. He didn't sound like the God who sent down fire to burn 450 prophets of Baal on Elijah's call. He didn't sound like the no-nonsense God their fathers worshipped. Who was

Herod to try to kill the Son of God? Yet all God said was *run*! Well, they obeyed, simply trusting. And life went on normally after that.

Time passed, the child grew, and Mary simply observed Him to see what unfolds. Then he turned 30-years-old and started His ministry. Again, Mary was following closely to see what will become of this miracle child that she gave birth to. She had been given a prophecy prior to His birth and she had watched closely to see how that would pan out. Many things had happened, but she was yet to see the "Saviour of the world" part of the prophecy. So, she kept her curiosity keen and watched closely for over 30 years.

However, three years down the line, she got the rudest shock of her whole life! The *Saviour of the world* and *Son of God* got killed by mere mortals! How could that happen? It certainly was a total deviation from what the angel told her on that fateful day when His conception was announced to her! Even worse, He died the most shameful and excruciating death ever! So, where was the *"He will be great, and will be called the Son of the Highest; and the Lord God will give Him the throne of His father David. And He will reign over the house of Jacob forever, and of His Kingdom there will be no end"* part of the prophecy she was told? (See Luke 1:32-33.)

Did God and His angel, Gabriel play an expensive joke on her? Had she been pranked? Was this the end? Well, yes, Jesus had told them He would rise again, but none of these playouts looked anything like what she was told. How exactly will He save the world or reign forever now that He was dead?

But you see, what God told Mary was *the end*, not *the process*. And that is His style. God never tells you the in-between of where you are and where He is taking you. He meets you where you are in the present and tells or shows you what He has prepared for you in the future, but He never tells you the process or the path. Therefore, faith is a necessity. By faith, we follow and trust Him to make good His word in our lives. This was what Mary understood that kept her going. Recall that she notably demonstrated this on two different occasions: the first was at the instance where the angel communicated God's counsel to her. She responded, *"Behold the maidservant of the Lord! Let it be to me according to your word"* (Luke 1:38). The second time was at the wedding in Cana where she told the servants, *"Whatever He says to you, do it"* (John 2:5). That's faith! This is where we must come to in our own lives as daughters of the King. We must learn to trust Him totally and completely. We must grow faith in His revealed word to us. God is too faithful to lie or fail on His promise. It is simply impossible! His word never returns to Him void without accomplishing what He sent it to do (Isaiah 55:11).

What has God Told You?

Blessed is she who believed, for there shall be a fulfilment of those things which were told her from the Lord.
– Luke 1:45

Her cousin, Elizabeth who she met to strengthen her faith in this new experience with the Lord said the words above to Mary. I believe Elizabeth must have learnt this experientially after seeing her husband turn dumb because he doubted what the angel told him from God. Whichever way, those words are as vital to us today as they were to Mary when they were first spoken. Performance of God's promises to you can answer only to your faith in His word to you. You can never have it any other way!

What has God said to you? I urge you to hold on to your faith in Him to bring to pass what He said. It does not matter how long it seems to be taking or what challenges you have had to endure; God is faithful. And if you can only trust Him some more, you will inevitably see His salvation. The vision is for an appointed time, and even if it seems to delay, wait for it, for it will surely come to pass (Habakkuk 2:3).

John 11:40, *"Jesus said to her, 'Did I not say to you that if you would believe you would see the glory of God?'"* Dear daughter of God, only believe! Believing births performance.

When the winds of struggles blow, keep His promises alive in your heart and they will strengthen you. They will guard your heart against giving in to the fads of the devil. They will fuel your faith. At such times, remind yourself of God's faithfulness to His word. If He has never failed anyone from time before creation, you will not be the first!

Chapter

FOUR

HER RELATIONSHIPS

The philosopher, Aristotle said man is a social animal; meaning, we thrive on relationships and social interactions. That is why the worst punishment or humiliation anyone can experience is to be locked away in a place where they never see or interact with another human being. It could be devastating to the point of losing one's mind.

We were created for interaction. God made sure of that from the time of creation. The Bible records that after God had created all things, including man, He saw that all other living creatures had counterparts of their own kinds except Adam. God had brought all creatures to Adam to name and hopefully find a suitable partner for necessary interaction, but he found none. *And the Lord God said, "It is not good that man should be alone; I will make him a helper comparable to him"* (Genesis 2:18). By this, God set a precedent for the necessity of relationships, not only marital, but generally. All humans thrive on relationships, which are of diverse kinds. But for our conversation in this book, I will dwell on the three essential relationships a woman must cultivate irrespective of the curves life has thrown at her.

Her Relationship with God

"...that the God of our Lord Jesus Christ, the Father of glory, may give to you

the spirit of wisdom and revelation in the knowledge of Him, the eyes of your understanding being enlightened; that you may know what is the hope of His calling, what are the riches of the glory of His inheritance in the saints, and what is the exceeding greatness of His power toward us who believe, according to the working of His mighty power which He worked in Christ when He raised Him from the dead and seated Him at His right hand in the heavenly places"
- Ephesians 1:17-20

Your relationship with God is the foundation of everything else about your life. A lack of a healthy relationship with and thorough knowledge/understanding of God will result in constant defeats in life. God created you, so He alone can best tell you about yourself and the life He designed you to live. Your knowledge of God empowers you to undertake great exploits on earth and to disappoint all negative expectations and labels that men set against you. Personally, my healing progressed as I grew in my knowledge of God. The more of Him I saw and learned of, the more of my true self I saw.

You see, the minute you got born again, everything about you changed in the spirit. But you must come to an understanding of the great exchange that happened in that instant in order to enter the reality of it and enjoy its benefits. That is what the Bible means when it talks about renewing our mind. And who else is better positioned to tell you what exactly happened when you got born again than the One who Himself executed the transformation!

My Turning Point

From the time my uncle and his wife separated, I became the dumping site for everyone's emotional trash and had no one who was truly accountable for me. Through time, I eventually found my own way of dealing with the countless episodes of pain, abuse and neglect. Those experiences left me feeling incompetent, inadequate, depressed and lonely. I avoided people and social situations because I didn't want to be judged or criticized. I found difficulty in speaking up; something I later discovered to be low self-esteem. This condition really held me back for many years and cost me several opportunities because I thought I wasn't good enough for anything. I believed that some people were just gifted for certain things but not others; until I attended a bible school and was told that I had the life of Christ on the inside of me. That made my chasing God to come to an end. I don't have to chase God. He found me and He resides in me. The thought that I now carry and house the very presence of God gave me chills. It took a while for it to sink in. All my years of service in church as a Christian, I always searched for God. I did so much to get His attention, His love, care and affection. And just the way I sought for my earthly father's attention, love and care and it was nowhere in view, I didn't see the love of God, neither did I feel His care and affection. I will say, of a truth, that I stayed a Christian because I didn't want to go to Hell. I couldn't bear to think about suffering eternally after the much suffering I had gone through here. That was the reason why I didn't go ahead with all the suicidal thoughts that plagued me. And who knows, perhaps a worse situation might have come to test my faith, like my atheist customer, and I would have been lost. Discovering the height, breadth, length, and depth of the love of God, which is Christ in me the hope of glory, changed my mind-set and my search of God's love for me ended. Christ's death, burial, resurrection and ascension are God's ultimate display of love for all mankind and me. It can never be quantified.

John 15:13 says, *"Greater love has no man than this, that a man should lay down his life for his friends."* I found out that He loves me just the way I am, even before the foundations of the earth were laid. Hallelujah! I am His daughter and a treasured heir. I carry His fullness inside me. Whenever the devil wants to put the thought of doubting God's love in my mind, I simply look on Christ, the express image of the invincible God. Knowing that I am royalty and I carry greatness began to restore a sense of self-worth in me. As I began the journey of self-discovery, which I call Christ-discovery, my confidence started building and my self-esteem started to improve. I took time to think of things that I was passionate about – activities that I enjoyed and was good at but had to give up due to unbelief, and as I engaged in them, I started to believe in myself again. Gradually, I started to understand that **my value does not decrease based on someone else's inability to see my worth** neither do the crushing circumstances of life that I went through diminish my worth. I discovered that my worth is solely founded in the life of Christ, solely in God, and because I am now living His life or He is living His life in me, I am worth more than anything on earth. I discovered that I am the King's daughter, and that my Father values me and treasures me deeply. It's all about DISCOVERY.

Likewise, right now, I want you too to start believing in yourself again, because you are worth more than they have made you to believe until now. It is my sincere hope and prayer that this book will launch you on a journey to understanding your self-worth. That you may understand how worthy you are, who you are, and the enormity of what you carry. You will discover that you alone are the most significant factor in how you feel about your life and your circumstances. Abraham Lincoln once said, *"It is difficult to make a man feel miserable when he feels worthy of himself."* You are worthy! You are worth the heart and life of Christ. You are *so* worthy! You deserve everything good in life.

See your present reality:

I have been crucified with Christ; it is no longer I who live, but Christ lives in me; and the life which I now live in the flesh I live by faith in the Son of God, who loved me and gave Himself for me. Galatians 2:20

When you receive Jesus into your life as Lord, a perfect union instantly occurs. You come into perfect oneness with Christ. You die to your old self and take on His own life, so that the life you live now is Christ living in and through you. Now, you no longer have a life of your own, but the life of Christ which He lives through you. The understanding of this truth set me free from the grip of my past. Once I understood that it was Christ's life I was living, I quit worrying about other people's opinions and expectations of me. What mattered was what the One whose life I am living thinks and says about me.

In truth, a relationship with Christ is a relationship with yourself. Knowing Christ is knowing you, since you are now in perfect union with Him. The more of Christ you know, the more of yourself you get to know.

Proverbs 23:7 says *as a man thinks in his heart, so is he.* You need to discover who you are and love yourself before you can give your best. Who are you? Who do you *think* you are? Many people do not know who they are, so they remain victims all their lives. Whether or not life is favourable and fair to you, your circumstances and experiences don't define who you are in Christ. You must learn of who you are in Christ through His word and build that knowledge into your consciousness so that it guides your thoughts and actions every day. I've made it a constant practice to always remind myself of who I am in Christ especially because growing up, I was called several derogatory names.

I must be deliberate to renew my mind and replace those old thoughts with only what God says about me. I choose to speak over myself what God says about me. Previously, I wallowed in depression, tears and moodiness, but I learned a new and better way to live – in victory. So, I stopped allowing other people's thoughts, opinions and actions to weigh me down. Instead, I walk with my head held up high as the King's daughter that I am, irrespective of what others think or say. My past doesn't define me anymore, but what my King-Father calls me, that is who I am. Yes, I am the King's precious daughter and I know it; so, I walk around with squared shoulders and springs under my feet because my Father owns everything you see and know. Hallelujah!

nowing God personally worked the miracle for me, and I have now embraced my newfound identity. I no longer log the names I was called. I am now everything God says I am, and that negates every word spoken against me in the past, the present, and the future. According to Philippians 2:5 says, *"Let this mind be in you which was in Christ Jesus"*. In other words, think like Christ; see yourself as Christ sees Himself and sees you. That is your path to constant victory. But it all starts with cultivating a constant relationship and fellowship with your Father every day. He longs for it; you should too.

HOW TO DEVELOP A THRIVING RELATIONSHIP WITH GOD

1. *You must be Born Again*

God is Spirit, and those who worship Him must
worship in spirit and truth.
– John 4:24
But the natural man does not receive the things of the Spirit
of God, for they are foolishness to him; nor can he know them,

because they are spiritually discerned.
– 1 Corinthians 2:14

Your relationship with God is very essential. Accepting Jesus as your lord and personal saviour brings you in union with Him. What manner of love the Father has given unto us, that we should be called the sons of God (1 John 4:7,8). If you will believe in your heart and confess with your mouth the Lord Jesus Christ, that He died, was buried and was resurrected, you shall be saved. As much as God wants to have a family relationship with the whole world, only those who believe in the Lord Jesus can He be a Father to.

2. *Study His Word and Meditate*

If the knowledge of Jesus is knowledge of yourself and Jesus is the word made flesh, then nothing else can teach you of Christ – and by extension, yourself – better than His word. His word should be your all-day craving. Make out time to study and interact with His word every day. The word renews our minds and reveals to us the things that have been freely given to us by our Father. God's word is a lamp to our feet and a light to our paths (Psalm 119:105). It is our guarantee for a life of perpetual victory, irrespective of what life throws at us. Get in the word and soak yourself with its truths about you. Let it dwell in you richly (1 Timothy 4: 13-16, Colossians 3:16). Meditation births understanding of the word in your spirit. The letter kills, but the Spirit gives life (II Corinthians 3:6). Reading God's word is not enough, you must spend ample time pondering on it to digest its truths and sink it into your subconscious mind. That is when victory is born. To meditate on the word means to concentrate your thoughts on it, asking questions and seeking answers. It is chewing on the word to crush out its nutrients to feed your spirit and renew your mind. This breed understanding, which in turn delivers to you your inheritance in Christ. It is the truth that you know and understand that works for you. Here, the eyes of your understanding get flooded with light to know the hope of His calling.

3.   *Pray*

When you have gained understanding of the word, then pray it into your life to deliver its power to bring about the changes you desire. Through prayer, we enforce what is ours by birth-right in Christ. We commune with God through prayer and obliterate the works of the devil – existing and intended – in our lives. In prayer, we speak to God as His children and He speaks back to us, giving us instructions and guidance for what we should do to further walk in our victory in Christ. Men ought to always pray and not to faint (Luke 18:1). It's not a call for debate, but an instruction. Therefore, prayer is a non-negligible practice for the child of God who would live in victory. The Bible says to pray without ceasing (I Thessalonians 5:17). Always praying in the Spirit helps you to build up your faith (Jude 20), and it's also an avenue to speak mysteries continuously to God. Make prayer your daily practice. It shows your trust and dependence on God to make good His word in your life.

4.   *Fellowship with other Believers*

This helps your growth in the things of God and further enhances your understanding of His ways. Do not neglect the assembling together of brethren (Hebrews 10:25), the Bible admonishes us. Fellowshipping with other believers where the truth of God's word is shared is very important to your faith in Christ. It builds you up spiritually, psychologically, socially, and otherwise. It provides you with a family of like minds that serve as a support system for your walk of faith. Don't neglect this no matter how busy your schedule might be.

5.   *Guard against Distractions*

This is one weapon the devil uses to draw us away from fellowshipping with God. He entices us with the lusts of the eyes and of the flesh, and the pride of life. These have always been his weapons. He lies to us that he can give us a good life outside God. That is what he did to Eve, promising to make her like God if she ate of the fruit God had instructed them not to eat (Genesis 3). The question is: who was she like at that instant? Didn't God say He created them in His image and likeness? Can you see the devil's deceptive tactic?

At other times, distractions can come to us as worrying over things that don't seem to be working in our lives. When you worry, you are telling God that you don't trust Him to be able to perform His promise to you. So, Jesus asked, "Which of you by worrying can add one cubit to his stature?" (Matthew 6:27). Have you ever pondered on that? In other words, worrying is an absolute waste of your time because it can never achieve anything for you. (Philippians 4:6). *"Be anxious for nothing, but in everything by prayer and supplication, with thanksgiving, let your requests be made known to God"*. So, let go and trust the One who can make happen the things you desire. Rest in His love for you. Don't ever let the devil talk you out of God's love. If he can't solve your problems (he only complicates them, according to John 10:10), then why should you listen to him?

Dear daughter of God, don't fall for the devil's lies and deceptions. He comes only to steal, kill and destroy. Only Jesus gives the abundant life. Stay with Him and grow your relationship with Him.

Her Relationship with Herself

"She remembered who she was and the game changed."
– Lalah Deliah

The woman who has discovered herself, her worth, her esteem, is unstoppable. She is like a freight train that is on full speed to its destination many miles away. The more you are at peace with your inner self, the more confidence you will exude in your daily life. You are self-aware and grounded in the knowledge of who you are in Christ. Your life is a reflection and representation of the very life of Christ who lives in you. You are a woman on a mission to affect her world for her Christ. When anyone meets you, they meet a different kind of woman – an empowered woman, and they leave richer than they came. You are a living spring of good, favour, and wellness. You exude radiant light that shines on both your paths and those of other people within your circle. You know your God and are empowered to do great exploits for His name and His Kingdom. He is your King-Father and you're pleased to do His biddings every day.

Dear woman, you must know yourself. You must make that journey to self-discovery. It changes everything. It redefines the game and puts you in the winning angle. Self-knowledge ignites your heart to believe in your power; and from that belief emerges your self-confidence. You know who you are. You know your power. You know who made you so. You are fierce, strong, and dynamic. You have a purpose and defined direction. You are on a journey for impact and fulfilment. You are the King's daughter. You are royal.

"But you are a chosen generation, a royal priesthood, a holy nation, His own special people, that you may proclaim the praises of Him who called you out of darkness into His marvellous light" (1 Peter 2:9)

You must learn to fellowship with yourself often. Spend time with your inner self. Ask yourself quality questions and endeavour to find answers to them. Questions like: Who am I? Why am I here? What was I sent here to do? What is my purpose and assignment? How much does God mean to me? What should I do today? Who can I be a blessing to right now? How can I better serve God's kingdom? Who can I encourage, support and uplift today, and how? Ask as many questions as come to mind and seek answers to them. Learn to enjoy your own company.

Yes, it is good to spend quality time interacting with other people, but you must ensure to spare time for yourself too. Spare time to just fellowship with yourself alone and meditate. That is how you will find and draw from your inner strength.

Let me quickly draw a line here. I am not talking about sitting in silence and musing over your predicaments and many challenges; that is the pathway to depression. No, I am rather talking about times when you affirm yourself despite the challenges you are faced with. Everybody goes through challenges in life, but it is those who learn how to rear their heads above the waters that eventually win and succeed. You must allocate time to chew on God's word about you. You must meditate day and night until the word takes root in your conscious and subconscious minds so that it becomes your default belief.

Few years ago, after I was already married, I fell into depression. Apparently, I was still trapped in my past, and the few expectations I had managed to muster as a young adult were not forthcoming. I was broken. I became a shadow of myself, only undertaking daily routines like a zombie. I prepared my family's meals, did the chores, prepared my boys for school, and everything else required of a woman, but I was dying inside. Two years into my marriage I started developing an addiction born out of pain and depression. All I did every day once everyone was out was watch TV. I became a fan of Telemundo and their many TV series. I followed perhaps every series they had on TV year in, year out until I finally couldn't take it anymore. I was tired and wanted out: out of everything – myself, marriage... life. I became a shadow of myself. I knew deep down that this wasn't me, but I couldn't get myself to let go of my pain, worries, and ultimately depression. The only way to blank out was to watch TV all day. I thought of many possibilities and options, including suicide, but somehow, I had some will to keep on. However, I did attempt to leave my marriage. But thank God that I found the courage to go seek counsel and prayer from my dear Mama, Pastor Opi Agha. Then, gradually, I began to find strength as I started to read God's word briefly every day.

By the turn of the following year, I decided to cut off from TV altogether. I told myself that I would use the January fasting and prayer period to fast off watching TV and see what happens. Truth be told, before the end of the fasting period, the appetite to sit by the TV died. Then I decided to devote my time and life to developing myself. I committed to studying God's word, listening to teachings, and reading great books. That was how I attained full, permanent victory over my past, my pain and depressive habits.

How to Develop Self-Love

Being in love with yourself builds your self-confidence and self-worth, and it will generally help you feel more positive about life. If you can learn to love yourself, you will be much happier and will learn how to best take care of yourself. When you are happy and truly in love with yourself, you will stop comparing yourself to others and will find yourself more confident, not worrying about what others think or expect of you. You will instead concern yourself with who God says you are and what He thinks of you.

Requirements for effective Self-Love

Forgive Yourself of Past Mistakes

Have you ever done something wrong and struggled to forgive yourself? Every time you think about it you regret ever embarking on that path. Forgive yourself of any mistakes you've made in the past no matter the gravity and whatever it cost you. This will empower you and give you a great feeling of incredible self-worth.

Forgive those that hurt you too. Forgiveness means to excuse someone from a fault or an offence. It entails renouncing anger or resentment against someone. It is a choice, which does not only favour the person that is guilty but favours also the person who chooses to forgive. *"Let all bitterness, wrath, anger, clamour, and evil speaking be put away from you, with all malice. And be kind to one another, tender-hearted, forgiving one another, even as God in Christ forgave you"* (Ephesians 4:31-32).

You are the only one that can hinder yourself from making progress in your life both physically and spiritually. You need to learn to forgive yourself and others.

1.   *Surprise Yourself sometimes*

Try things out – even things out of your control. Say yes to things you would not normally say yes to. This will even help you with getting to know yourself better. You may find out that you enjoy things you never realized or tried before. Try and get out of your comfort zone and see what happens. Interestingly, oftentimes it will most likely be positive. Try activities like hiking, dancing, sports, gyming, bawling, vacation trips, skydiving, visiting historic places or art galleries, karaoke night-outs, etc. Anything that makes you tick.

2.   *Say No to People sometimes*

Focus on yourself when you can, or if you are overwhelmed. The ability to say "No" is a hallmark of maturity and self-awareness. It does not make you a bad person as society tries to make us feel many times. If it is not convenient for you or it does not fit into your schedule, politely but firmly say no and mean it.

I grew up wanting to please everyone; I sought to be approved by all, and this eventually took its toll on me by sinking me further into bitterness and hatred. I give my very last to see others happy. I go miles to ensure no one around me is sad, hungry or neglected, no matter the cost, even when I'm exhausted. But it often turns out that the very people you lose yourself to please do not even recognise or appreciate your effort instead, they despise you. I have been in so many situations where I was left alone with no one to cheer me up. Everyone thinks you are so strong and have everything in abundance; you don't have any need in the world. I couldn't say no to anyone. But one day, someone dear to me, whom I always helped whenever she called, requested for a thing that I didn't have at the time, and I told her. I made attempts to offer a substitute, but this person refused. Instead, she became so angry and bitter that I refused to grant her request. She went about telling everyone who cared to listen. That was an eye opener for me. People could really be selfish. Most people don't care about you no matter what you do or don't do. Just do as the Holy Spirit leads you, and you should not try to displease yourself to please someone. The most the person can do is to be angry with you, but you will have a clear conscience and feel good for not displeasing yourself to please another person.

3.   *Pursue New Interests*

It's great to try something new that you have wanted to try for a while or have been too scared to do. Speaking before a crowd — large or small — gives me goose pimples, but I am trying to challenge myself to do more of it now. I constantly tell myself that there's nothing to be afraid of. And when opportunity shows up, I take it and do it despite my fears. I know it is part of my calling, so I must build myself into it, starting small. Try out new interests and go for the things your heart yearns to do. You will elevate your positive feeling of yourself faster that way. Yes, do it afraid. Soon the fear will dissipate.

4.   *Challenge Yourself*

You will never know what you're capable of achieving unless you try. And if you fail, learn from it and go again until you get it. No one was born an expert at what they do today; people build and develop themselves by challenging their previous limits. Dare to dream and to pursue it. Life makes way for the daring heart that refuses to settle for small!

Dealing with the Past

In truth, a woman has not come into the place of wisdom until she has learnt to heal from the hurts and pains of her past and has thrown away the baggage she has carried for many years. You see, like me, many women go into marriage the wrong way. We carry a lot of invisible baggage filled with mistakes and hurts of past years into our matrimonial homes. And then we wonder why we can't find happiness in our new homes. The answer is simple: you relate with your husband from a mind-frame of your past experiences. You don't even realize you are doing that, but it steals away your potential joy in the home. Sometimes, you wall yourself in so hard and become impenetrable to your husband. No matter how hard he tries, you subconsciously don't let him in. He is at a loss for why you respond to him the way you do with hostility and lack of affection, yet you sometimes don't even realize that you are responding in such a manner towards him.

Your past is keeping you trapped, dear sister, and it is equally stealing away your today. Why should you allow an experience to rob you twice? It did in the past, and now again in your present; all because you allow it. But no more! You must denounce your past right now. Let it go and refuse to be held back. You can't lose yesterday and lose today as well. In fact, if you don't stop it now, it will follow you into your tomorrow and still mess it up. God forbids! Why should you give away such power to an experience that should be left where it rightly belongs: *in your past*? I charge you to let go now. No matter how bad it still hurts...let it go. In fact, the reason it hurts is because you have refused to let it go. You have held on to it in your heart and secretly justified holding on to it. You have subtly enjoyed how it makes you feel like a victim. You have allowed your past to convince you that you are powerless, and you have accepted it and pitched your tent there. Lying devil!

Life comes with its many hurdles and consequences in form of pain, hurt, rejection, betrayal, disease, shame, lack, loss, deprivation, condemnation, doubts, fear, etc. I used to think the issues of my past were peculiar to me. I grew up never imagining or believing that someone else could be going through what I went through. But as scriptures declare, "No trial has overtaken you that is not faced by others..." (1 Corinthians 10: 13).

So therefore, permit me to say everyone has a story from the past or present that has in one way or the other crippled our minds and limited our actions. It is impossible to hide it when you are crippled inside because it limits you on the outside.

A lot of us define ourselves by our issues and pains rather than who God says we are. The truth is, if your issues identify you for a time, you tend to forget who you are. For instance, in the scriptures we find,
- The woman with the issue of blood
- The demoniac
- The adulterous woman
- The Samaritan woman
- The deaf man
- The blind man, etc.

All these were individuals whose names we do not know because they were identified by their issues. Whenever we allow things and people to dictate our lives, there is an identity crisis. We live with a broken identity. If you are ever going to walk in victory and dominion, you must define yourself by who the King of kings says you are. You are designed for the Godkind of life and experiences. Irrespective of what your past story is, you are the King's daughter. You have been set up on high where only eagles soar, thrive and feast. You have been accepted in the Beloved. The truth is that God loves you, and in Him is the ability to be healed from every pain and hurt of life. Whether you contributed to the many troubles you have faced so far in life or not, God has never stopped loving you and He can never stop. He loved you from start, long before you were born with an everlasting love. He created you, His daughter, as an eternal excellency, the joy of many generations. You are special to God, the eternal King; You mean everything to Him and for Him. He gives you an unbroken and buoyant identity.

People with issues tend to want to be accepted the way they are. They want to be
- Affirmed
- Comforted in their state
- Pitied and encouraged to remain where they are

For a long time, that was me. I was completely broken and shattered. I hoped and trusted that everyone around me would understand me. People complained about the fact that I was secluded and unsocial and all I could say was, that is who I am. Excuse me, were we born bitter, negative, depressed, unsocial, etc? No, life made us that way.

Many of you reading this now have been knocked down by life. You have gone through experiences that have long passed, but still, the vestiges thereof are lingering in your mind till now. You have been held back and held down by the past for too long. It is time, get up and move forward.

A story in the Bible that perfectly illustrates this point with much clarity comes to my mind. It is the story of the man at the pool of Bethesda, captured in John 5:1-15. He had been lying down with other invalids for 38 years, crippled by an experience that had refused to let go of him. 38 years is such a long time to stay trapped! Can you imagine being in the same spot, waiting in pain and agony for your turn to receive a miracle, for a changed life, for 38 years? That's certainly unthinkable to most people. Yet, many of us live like that. We see the person we aspire to become but we refuse to stretch for it. We see the books we could have written but are limited in our minds. We hear songs we could have composed but can't bear to think of it. We see lives we could have impacted with our own lives and story, but we don't have a voice to speak out. We see places we could have visited but we don't have the legs to move. Souls we could have won through evangelism, but we tell ourselves that everyone fights their own battles.

Jesus came to this man and straight away asked him: Do you want to be healed? He must have been angry with Jesus for not feeling pity for him. Notice that Jesus didn't ask, *"What's wrong with you? How long have you been here?"* or questions in the same line of thought. He didn't care to ask; He just knew all of that was not going to improve the situation. What was necessary was the crippled man's willingness to change his life for good.

Yes, terrible things happen – you've been through a rape, a bad divorce, rejection, you grew up poor and deprived, aggrieved, sick, molested, abused (physical, emotional and sexual). It's all not your fault. You didn't do anything wrong to deserve it, and surely no form of abuse should be glossed over. You expect good people to understand where you have been and what you have had to endure. You want to hear them say sorry and indulge your tendency to pity-party. Now, they may tolerate your disposition maybe for the first week, first month or first year, but when it has prolonged to years of self-pity, depression and feeling of loneliness, soon you are not different from the multitudes at the pool. Bad things do happen, but how you respond to them defines your character and the quality of your life. You can choose to sit in perpetual sadness, immobilized by the gravity of your loss or you can choose to rise from the pain and treasure the most precious gift you have, which is life itself!

All the things you went through as a child tend to put you on the pedestal of unforgiveness, bitterness, anger, shame, and guilt. You can either spend the rest of your life staying there and blaming whoever caused you pain and agony, maybe your family, friends, society, the church, etc. or embrace the healing that comes from Jesus Christ.

The crippled man replied Jesus by saying; *"I have no one to help me into the pool. Even when I'm trying to get in after the stirring, someone else reaches in before me."* This sounds like a man who had already given up on life and lost all hope of ever recovering. At this point he was full of bitterness, anger and blame. But Jesus says, *"Get up, pick up your mat and walk."* In other words, change your perspective to life; change your mind-set. Get up, pick up what was carrying you and begin to step into your fullness. **When you get up, you get out.** You gain access to things and places you thought were beyond your reach before. Therefore, get up and walk into the place of your potential. They don't come to meet you; you walk to them.

If you remain on your back, greatness, achievements, impact will not come knocking. We need to understand that healing comes with responsibility: GET UP, PICK UP, AND WALK.

Tell yourself: I'm done staying in this position of blame. I am not blaming anything or anyone for my predicaments anymore. I choose to get up, pick up myself from the self-pity state and showcase my experiences to the glory of Jesus, thereby fulfilling my purpose.

You are *not* powerless, but powerful beyond measure. Yes, you have thought about letting go many times, but fear gripped your heart. You've been in this so long that you have forgotten how it feels to be free, so you are afraid of what you are unsure of. Nevertheless, that is not what you are most afraid of; it is something else: according to Marianne Williamson:

> *Our deepest fear is not that we are inadequate. Our deepest fear*
> *is that we are powerful beyond measure. It is our light, not our darkness,*
> *that most frightens us. We ask ourselves, who am I to be brilliant, gorgeous,*
> *talented and fabulous? Actually, who are you not to be? You are a child of*
> *God.*
> *Your playing small doesn't serve the world. We were born to make manifest*
> *the glory of God that is within us. It's not just in some of us; it's in everyone.*
> *And as we let our own light shine, we unconsciously give other people*
> *permission*
> *to do the same. As we are liberated from our own fear, our presence*
> *automatically*
> *liberates others.*

Therefore, the devil is afraid of your liberation, because your presence will automatically liberate others, starting with your family. However, only you and God have the final say over your life. It's time to change the game, sister. Nothing can stop a woman who has discovered who she is in Christ and knows that she is the King's daughter.

Her Relationship with Other People

*"The world needs strong women. Women who will lift and build others,
who will love and be loved. Women who live bravely, both tender and fierce.
Women of indomitable will.*
– Amy Tenney

Women are especially relational. They know what they want and go for it. They are strong and of an indomitable will to live and to thrive. They are strong, tender, and fierce. They add flavour to the world.

Women understand that people are different and unique, and they seek to understand each person and relate with them appropriately. Strong women are humble and teachable. They are naturally open to learning and growth.

Strong women are emotionally intelligent and mature. They try to manage their emotions when it comes to dealing with other people. They understand that life cannot be lived in isolation, and no matter how bad people make them feel and how many times they get hurt, they somehow find the will to get up, dust themselves, and keep going. The world needs strong women who have discovered themselves and their unique flavours and are not afraid to be different; women who try even after failing many times. They always find a way to pick up the pieces and continue their journey to destiny fulfilment. The question is: are you a strong woman or a weakling who chickens out of life's fighting ring? Do you stand up for what you know to be right or do you sit back and wallow in your seemingly unfortunate circumstances? Do you not realize that those challenges come to you because you are empowered already to confront and daunt them instead of the other way around? Do you not realize that you are more than you think and have believed of yourself until now? You are not what the world has sought to make you believe of yourself, but you are a strong woman on a mission to the place of purpose, and only *you* can stop *you* through the things *you* permit to be perpetuated in your life. You are a winner, more than a conqueror. Yes, that's who you are, not a wimp.

You ought, therefore, to be confident, tenacious and strong. Be dynamic and accommodating, but not naïve. Deal with people based on their uniqueness, difference and relevance in your life, and you will thrive. Understand that everyone plays a different role in your life, which you must decode and learn to deal with appropriately, because you are endowed with the wisdom of your Father. You are the King's daughter... remember?

Chapter

FIVE

HER HERITAGE

The English dictionary defines the word 'heritage' as "that which is inherited; a title or property or estate that PASSES BY LAW TO THE HEIR on the death of the owner" (emphasis mine). This means that heritage is anything that is inherited *legally by an heir* after the death of the progenitor or parent. So, to bring us into the God-class lifestyle through our defined identity, I want us to explore some of our inheritances in God, our King-Father, in this chapter.

The Bible says that *a good man leaves an inheritance to his children's children* (Proverbs 13:22), and we know without doubt that God *is* good, as the Bible repeatedly affirms. Therefore, as a good Father who honours and upholds His word, it is impossible for God to have left us without an inheritance, especially since He has fulfilled the legal precondition of death through His Son Jesus. In addition, following the death of Jesus, God's written will has bequeathed all His possessions to us as His heirs, as shown in the verses below:

Christ has redeemed us from the curse of the law, having become a curse for us (for it is written, "Cursed is everyone who hangs on a tree"), that the blessing of Abraham might come upon the Gentiles in Christ Jesus, that we might receive the promise of the Spirit through faith.
– Galatians 3:13-14

The Spirit Himself bears witness with our spirit that we are children of God, and if children, then heirs—heirs of God and joint heirs with Christ, if indeed we suffer with Him, that we may also be glorified together.
– Romans 8:16-17

The scriptures above establish one fact: *you and I are heirs of God and qualify for His inheritance.* Following the sin of Adam and Eve in the garden of Eden, all humanity was cut off from direct access to the rich treasures of God's kingdom because we were disconnected from God as our Father. And because we were not His legal children, by divine order we could not enjoy all that He had for us. We became slaves to the devil. But thank God for Jesus who came and took our place in a spiritual judicial exchange that secured our liberty to become children of God again. And because Jesus fulfilled the ultimate price for our sins, which is spiritual death – disconnection from God, and conquered the devil in it, you and I have now been adopted and engrafted into God as His children and heirs. We now qualify for His inheritance, which He has bequeathed to us.

In Him also we have obtained an inheritance, being predestined according to the purpose of Him who works all things according to the counsel of His will, that we who first trusted in Christ should be to the praise of His glory.
– Ephesians 1:11-12

The land you have given me is a pleasant land. What a wonderful inheritance!
– Psalm 16:6, NLT

As we all know, God *cannot* lie. So, we are not only God's daughters and heirs, but He has given us *all things that pertain to life and godliness* (II Peter 1:3), equipping us for our greatness irrespective of what our past experiences may look like.

When Jesus died in our stead, He made a public show of the devil's eternal defeat, which concurrently secured our eternal liberation from his power. Now he is beneath us; only that we do not know, so we remain under his influence by allowing him to control our actions and realities through deception.

Man, that is in honour, and understandeth not, is like the beasts that perish.
- Psalms 49:20, KJV

I realize that the greatest undoing of many Christians is ignorance. Little wonder, God exclaimed that His people are destroyed for lack of knowledge (Hosea 4:6). Also, the prophet Daniel affirmed that it is the people who *know* their God (and who they are in Him) that shall be strong and do exploits (Daniel 11:32).

In truth, the reason many of us have had our identities in Christ corroded for so long is our lack of knowledge of who God has made us in Himself and the immense rights, privileges and responsibilities that we have received as children of the King. Therefore, we live beneath our true identities, as the scripture above asserts, instead of royalty that we are! We are heirs of God, the King of the Universe. We are royalty – **Kings** (Revelation 1:6). Oh, I pray that we would all grasp the richness of these words and the power that they convey!

A common adage states, *"What you do not know is bigger than you"*. Well, I say that what you don't know, you can never grasp or walk in the reality of. It takes knowledge and understanding of your person and position in God to step into the realities of your adoption as a daughter of the King.

The devil thrives on your ignorance to keep you subjugated to his evil vagaries. God says you are a god in His class, created in His image and likeness. Thus, you ought to live above the elements of this world. In other words, if you take stock of your current experiences and find that your reality is contrary to this, the missing link is apt knowledge of who you are in Christ, your god-status. You were designed for the Godkind of life and experiences. Irrespective of what your past story is, now that you have come into Christ and become the King's heir, you have been set up on high where only eagles soar, thrive and feast. You have been accepted in the Beloved and made to sit together with Christ in heavenly places. You have left the realm of ordinary, repressive experiences and have been elevated into God's kind of experiences, where only peace, health, wellness, prosperity, and the good life are the norm. This is your precious heritage in Christ.

The Conveyer of our Inheritance

As we have seen already, our inheritance is a done deal with God. He completed the transaction when Jesus died on our behalf. The ball is now in our court to take possession of what is ours. We must stand up to the devil, look him in the eye and toss his baggage of corroded identity back at him. But it takes knowledge to do this and to take possession of what is now legally yours in Christ. You must quit living in perpetual darkness and at the enemy's mercy. Thank God for His glorious light which illuminates us!

Our inheritance is conveyed to us through the revelation of God's word in our spirit. The principle of God's kingdom is such that what you don't know or what you don't have a revealed understanding of will continue to elude you, according to Ephesians 1:17-18:

That the God of our Lord Jesus Christ, the Father of glory may give to you the Spirit of wisdom and revelation in the knowledge of Him (through His word), *the eyes of your understanding being enlightened; that you may know what is the hope of His calling, what are the riches of the glory of His inheritance in the saints.* (Emphasis mine)

Apostle Paul carried a burden, which was for the church to know what has been given to them. And it became his prayer always. When we know that we carry His fullness on the inside of us and all that pertains to this life has been given to us, we will start to rejoice and celebrate. We will worry no more and instead be grateful always. You see, the scripture says everything has been given unto us through the *knowledge of HIM* that has called us to glory and virtue. This means that everything we would ever need in this life and beyond can only be obtainable through the knowledge of Jesus Christ who has glorified us.

Revelation and understanding of Jesus Christ is the precondition for knowing what are yours in God and taking possession of them. And this revelation, stemming from God's word, is what delivers your inheritance to you.

So now, brethren, I commend you to God and to the word of His grace, which is able to build you up and give you an inheritance among all those who are sanctified.
– Acts 20:32

Let us now itemize and learn some of our inheritances in God.

1. Heritage of Eternal Life

For God so loved the world that He gave His only begotten Son, that whoever believes in Him should not perish but have everlasting life.
– John 3:16

This is where the journey starts. The journey starts with you becoming the King's heir by receiving His very life into your spirit. And this is made possible only after you receive the sacrifice of Jesus on your behalf. Looking back at my own life, my transformation started when I received Jesus into my heart in my first year of secondary school as I earlier shared. That was the turning point for me. Though it seemed like nothing significantly changed after that experience, but in retrospect, everything changed indeed. All that I am today is hinged on that one experience of turning myself over to the Lord and becoming the King's own daughter, delightsome, loved and cherished by His super large heart.

God's eternal life in your spirit is what opens the door for you to enjoy everything else. His eternal life makes you righteous and qualified in His sight. Therefore, if you are reading this and haven't had the glorious experience of receiving Jesus into your heart, then you really haven't started the journey to finding your true, unbroken identity yet. The reason is simple: your true identity is found *only* in Jesus. Hence, I invite you to evaluate your life right now and make the best decision you will ever make, which is to invite Jesus into your heart and become His daughter. Receive His eternal life today and start your journey to healing and rediscovering your truest identity. Just repent of your sins right now in sincere prayer and receive Him as your Lord and Saviour. Say this prayer...

Lord Jesus, I invite You into my heart today and ask You to be my Lord and Saviour from this day forward. I repent of all my sins and submit to Your Lordship. Change my life and make me brand new again, as Your Spirit comforts and heals me. Help me to walk in Your will every day. Amen!

2. Heritage of Peace

These things I have spoken to you, that in Me you may have peace.
In the world you will have tribulation; but be of good cheer,

I have overcome the world.
– John 16:33

Notice Jesus didn't promise us a tribulation-free life, because we live in an imperfect world and the devil is still on rampage to detract as many people from God's purpose for their lives, if they permit him by being ignorant. However, Jesus bequeathed His surpassing peace to us hinged on the assurance that we have already overcome all tribulations in Him. Therefore, we are victorious even before the challenges come. Hallelujah!

Therefore, a person may seem to have all of hell let loose on them and still be unperturbed by the precarious circumstances. What happens is that the peace of God guards and garrisons their heart against worrying. They understand that worrying changes nothing. They are assured in God that their light afflictions are but for a moment and working for them a far more exceeding weight of glory. They have learned and trained their minds to heed the advice in I Peter 5:6-9 which says:

Therefore, humble yourselves under the mighty hand of God, that He may exalt you in due time,
Casting all your care upon Him, for He cares for you.
Be sober, be vigilant; because your adversary the devil walks about like a roaring lion, seeking whom he may devour.
Resist him, steadfast in the faith, knowing that the same sufferings are experienced by your brotherhood in the world.

Dear friend, you must come to the place of trust in the peace of God to guard your heart through whatever challenges you may be confronted with per time. You must always remember that challenges come to try our faith in God, and after we persevere, we will enjoy the ultimate promise of the word God spoke to us.

And the peace of God [that peace which reassures the heart, that peace] which transcends all understanding, [that peace which] stands guard over your hearts and your minds in Christ Jesus [is yours].
– Philippians 4:7, AMP

3. Heritage of Prosperity

Let them shout for joy and be glad, who favor my righteous cause; and let them say continually, "Let the Lord be magnified, who has pleasure in the prosperity of His servant."
– Psalm 35:27

Prosperity is your heritage and birth-right in God. God takes pleasure in your prosperity, never in your lack or poverty. I don't care what you have been taught or what you have believed before now, poverty does not glorify God. It never has and never will.

Prosperity, as used here, is an all-encompassing word. It should not be perceived as being financial alone, but also as it affects our mental, physical, social and spiritual life – which is the totality of man. When you increase in knowledge, you tend to act better, affecting every area of your life. The Bible says we have the mind of Christ. Every one of us is good at one thing or the other. But whatever area you know you have prospered in should be a tool with which you reach out to your world. Many await the shining of your light to see their own paths clearly. For instance, speaking, acting, teaching, singing, writing, selling, etc. are few of the areas in which you can release the wealth that has been embedded on your inside. When you lack in an area, it means you need to acquire more knowledge in that area and work at it. So long as you are willing to put in the work, that's all; you have what it takes to prosper at it.

Furthermore, financial poverty does not make people humble and simple-hearted, just as wealth does not make people haughty or arrogant. Money simply is a faithful agent that reveals who you are at your core. If you love money (which the Bible warns against), you will lie, cheat and scheme to get it – whether you are poor or rich. And when you are rich, the love of money will make you reckless, arrogant and abusive to others. Thus, the presence or lack of money only reveals who a man truly is. Knowing and trusting that wealth will be to you a tool for fulfilling purpose, God made sure to include it in the salvation package. Therefore, imbibe the excellent mind-set that your King-Father wants you to prosper so that you can reach and affect more people with His love, and expect to be prosperous in the works of your hands. Yes, God prospers us by bringing us into favour and blessing the works of our hands. He commands the blessing in our storehouses so that we are filled and able to be a blessing to others.

Never forget also that the purpose of the prosperity (spiritual, mental, financial, social, academic and physical) God brings into your life is to enable you to reach out to the world around you – your domain (as we'll see in the next chapter). Everything God blesses you with, after you have been comforted by it, should be a tool of blessing to other people. This is why God prospers us.

Again proclaim, saying, 'Thus says the Lord of hosts: "My cities shall again spread out through prosperity; the Lord will again comfort Zion, and will again choose Jerusalem."
– Zechariah 1:17

I have the privilege of hosting periodic outreach meetings for less privileged people, especially women in the communities near me; and I cannot begin to convey to you the immense awe that comes with the feeling of knowing that God is using you to solve another person's needs. God's blessings are not to be hoarded, but to be released as a blessing to other people. Please never forget this.

4. Heritage of Health and Long Life

With long life I will satisfy him, and show him My salvation.
– Psalm 91:16

As the King's heir, it is not part of your heritage to die young or to suffer ill health, frequenting the hospital. No, you have a covenant of preservation with your Father, the King. You only need to understand and appropriate what is yours already.

Aside being the King's heir, you are His representative on earth. You are a woman on a divine assignment, a mandate that must be achieved to advance God's kingdom here. And the One who sent you knows that you need health, energy and vitality to consistently follow through on your assignment and to finish the race committed to you before passing on the baton. Therefore, He is committed to keeping you in good health so long as you play your part.

You play your part essentially in two ways: by constantly confessing your heritage of divine health in God and by taking good care of your health through good dieting and regular exercise. I joined a hiking group and a dancing group some time ago and, believe me, it was one of the most exhilarating experiences I have ever had. Of course, it was a stretch for me, especially the first time I joined them to hike; my whole body was sore for many days. But aside the surge of joy I felt when we reached the top of the hill, it generally made me feel better in my body. It was intense exercise for me, and I started to feel my energy level pumping up. I also do regular brisk walking around the house. All these are exercises I need to do to keep my health in shape for the assignment the Master has given me.

I encourage you to imbibe the habit of regular exercises. It will do you much good. You may not join a hiking or dance group like I did. You can simply do routine jogging or brisk walking or register at a gym – whatever is convenient for you for a start. More importantly, commit to it. Also, do not forget to keep the confession of your heritage of divine health on your lips every day.

How to Possess and Maximize Your Heritage in God
1.   Be Conscious of What is Yours
This Book of the Law shall not depart from your mouth, but you shall
meditate in it day and night, that you may observe to do according to
all that is written in it. for then you will make your way prosperous,
and then you will have good success.
– Joshua 1:8

You must believe God's word hook, line and sinker. You must accept its truths as your present reality. You must believe that you are precisely who God says you are in His word. You must guard and garrison your heart with these truths through constant meditation.

To possess, maximize and fully enjoy your heritage in Christ every day, you must build them into your everyday consciousness and awareness. Soak your mind with these truths so that they easily ooze out of you every time the devil tries to bring contrary realities your way. That way, you will easily refute his offering and superimpose God's truth instead.

Learn to meditate on these truths every day so that you can keep them at the fore of your mind. Then confess them over your life as well. Our world was created by God's word and still responds to it, so speak what God says over your life consistently. One way to help you stay consistent with this is to hang scriptural truths in places where you can easily see them every day. Examples are beside your bed, on a board in your office, on your dressing mirror, on your refrigerator, etc. These will help to etch them in your consciousness and thereby appropriate them in your life.

2.   *Exercise Your Faith*

Faith is built on your level of obedience. Remember what Mary said to the servants at the wedding in Cana: "*Whatever He says to you, do it*" (John 2:5). The verse summarizes faith.

To exercise your faith means to take obedient actions based on what you believe from God's word. Take the story of the woman with the issue of blood in Mark 5:25-34 as a case in point. This woman must have heard of the miracle-working power of Jesus and the many healings that other people had received, and she believed in her heart that if she could only touch the helm of Jesus' garment she would be healed. Then she acted on that belief, exercised her faith, and got her healing instantly.

Therefore, it's not enough to meditate on the word and stay conscious of it, act based on what has been revealed to you and expect results. God cannot lie! He will always uphold the integrity of His word.

3.   *Improve on Your Attitude and Character*

A common axiom asserts that *attitude is everything*. Also, your character is a major consideration for enjoying favour through men. God blesses us through people, and these people don't see your heart or good intentions. What they see are your attitude and character, which informs their disposition towards helping you. Thus, you must pay keen attention to these.

While you are being conscious of your heritage in Christ, give diligence to improving your character and attitude towards people. Improve on your timeliness with appointments, be empathetic and compassionate towards people, be diligent on your job or with your business, be excellent and professional at what you do, be cheerful and friendlier towards people, be reliable and trustworthy, etc. You can't even begin to imagine what doors of opportunities these can open for you if you imbibe them.

As an employer of labour, I have had instances where I put out job vacancies and got calls from interested persons whose primary concern was how much the salary will be. Already, such a person has lost the job opportunity. Why? They've just told me their priority – money, not value addition. Again, attitude and character are everything.

4. *Watch Your Network*

Immediately Mary was told of the impossible thing God was about to do with and through her, to empower her faith, she quickly went to associate with Elizabeth who was already a living testimony of the impossibility-crushing power of God. Likewise, you must be deliberate to find and associate with people who will bolster your faith in God, especially with respect to the things God is telling and showing you.

Evil company corrupts. If your network does not believe the same things as you, you are in the wrong company; change it quickly.

Chapter

SIX

HER DOMAIN

As this book gradually draws to a close, it is critically important that we discuss the place of power and authority. That is, after you have recovered from your hitherto broken identity and received healing from the pain of your past, what should you do henceforth? How should you channel this new found energy and power in Christ? Now that you know who you are and what power resides inside you, how should you channel and maximize it, and to what end? What is your assignment as the King's daughter and how should you go about executing it? I call this *Your Domain*.

The English Dictionary defines 'domain' as a territory over which rule or control is exercised. This means that your domain is the territory over which God has given you influence and a measure of control. This could be at home in your family, on your job, in your neighbourhood or community, in the market segment where your business operates, etc. Your domain is any place where your King-Father has placed you at a given time and expects you to harness His investments in you towards pointing other people to His love. Your domain is your empowerment for kingdom service. It is your place of power.

Finding Your Power

All through the Bible, everyone who stood out in their generation and truly served God's purpose for their lives first came to a realization and an understanding of their person and placement with God. That is always the starting point. God first calls us to Himself through consecration; then He equips us for the assignment He has designed for us. Then He sends us to be and to effect the change He wants to make happen through us in the world. In other words, everyone has an assignment in God, a place of dominion and power, a place of authority. It is a place that is designed to bring you into significance, not just fame; a place where you are equipped to make a difference, where your life becomes impactful.

Esther serves as a perfect illustration of this principle, specifically, her stepping up and speaking up for the Jews who were slated for destruction. Esther would have just been another queen, not different from many before her and many after her, except for this singular act. She would have been known only – if at all she got a trans-generational mention – as the Jewish girl who became the queen of the world in her day. However, her story is different now because her life became significant when she chose to heed Mordecai's advice and step up to the aid of the Jewish nation.

He sent back this answer: "Do not think that because you are in the king's house you alone of all the Jews will escape. For if you remain silent at this time, relief and deliverance for the Jews will arise from another place, but you and your father's family will perish. And who knows but that you have come to your position for such a time as this?"

– Esther 4:13-14, NIV

Oh, thank God for men like Esther's uncle, Mordecai, who understood divine principles and could discern the times. He was instrumental in moving Esther from the place of silence as a queen, seen but not heard, to her place of significance and dominance. Were it not for Mordecai, Esther would probably have been isolated from the need she was raised to meet. She would have lost her voice and her opportunity for rising to significance forever. Every one of us needs a Mordecai in our lives sometimes, and I pray to God that this book will be that "Mordecai" for you.

We all need people who remind us – especially at critical times – what God's assignment is for our lives and why we must endeavour to undertake it irrespective of how we feel about the prevailing circumstances. Everything you have been through so far and everything you have achieved were God's equipment for your assignment, to occupy your domain and exert your authority in God.

The Crippling Effect

Many times, the enemy's weapon of choice to keep us from stepping into our place of assignment and purpose is *fear*. Fear is what he uses to cripple us and hold us back. In Esther's case, it was the fear of death by the king's decree. I imagine her heart cringing with fear as thoughts about the possibility of a death sentence if she went to the king uninvited filled her mind. The devil must have reminded her of Vashti and told her that Vashti's case was even better than what will happen to her. At least Vashti was still alive, whereas she won't even see another sunlight if she tried it. He must have painted ugly pictures in her mind in one split second. That is his age-long method, which is why the Bible instructs us to "*put on the whole armour of God that you may be able to withstand the wiles of the enemy*" (Ephesians 6:12). That is all the devil has: *schemes of deceit* and *bluffs*, to get you to doubt God's word to you and His power to do the impossible for and through you. Fear is a crippler.

I remember my earliest experience with fear as a child. I may have been between ages 5 and 6 then. An older girl in my neighbourhood would bully, abuse and molest me every time she saw me; I mean *every single time*. She seemed to derive pleasure from it. And the more I obliged her, the more her power over me grew. Every time I went out to play and she was there or met me, she would bully me by taking whatever was mine, stopping me from playing with the other kids, asking me to leave, etc. I was so afraid of her. Every time I saw her, I would cringe in fear. And of course, she wouldn't stop – since she seemed to be enjoying the feeling she got from my subservience to her.

It went on for about a year or so, until one day when I was really having fun playing with some kids in the neighbourhood and she came around. As usual, she immediately commanded that I let go of the swing and leave. I did at first but came back just as I started to walk away. I stood and told her she could do whatever she wanted to, I didn't care, and I wasn't leaving. Even now, as I think about it, I still can't fathom where such boldness came from. Maybe I was too pained by the fact that my fun time on the swing was abruptly cut short for no just cause. Well, whatever it was, my bully of about a year was shocked to her bone and her face showed it; but the more interesting thing is that she literally did nothing – not beat me, not shout at me, nothing. And that was the last time she ever threatened me again. I "bought" my freedom by simply standing up to her and refusing to allow fear to get the better of me.

Isn't this exactly what happened with Esther? When she refused to yield to the devil's suggestions in her head, but followed her uncle's wise counsel, she stepped into her place of purpose and secured deliverance for God's people.

Fear has been aptly described as *false evidence appearing real*. In other words, fear is a mirage; a tool the devil uses to keep us grounded when we allow him. But no more! Shake off that fear right now and step into your domain of greatness in God! Begin to dig out Gods instruction for you and run with it. God is counting on you for souls, revivals, changes and shifts on the earth.

The Ultimate Target

It was not long ago that God revealed to me that all the while my voice was the devil's target. Because of my crippled identity following my many hostile experiences as a child, my voice, which is supposed to be my strength, weapon and power, was lost. When I say voice, I literally mean relevance in life, being a change agent, and living a life of impact.

The experiences I went through crippled my identity. I didn't have a clue who I was or where my life was headed. Depression and suicidal thoughts became the order of the day. I hated myself and didn't see anything good in me. I didn't want to be known. I didn't want to know anyone. I preferred to be left alone all day. I didn't want to be bothered or to bother anyone.

People would tell me that I was beautiful, but when I looked in the mirror I saw otherwise. Then I would wonder what they were looking at or if their eyes were working well at all. I also had trust issues and could not trust anyone with anything. Whenever anyone said he or she loved me, I immediately put up a wall to guard against pain. I had been inundated by pain and too many hurts that I wanted nothing to do with anyone who claimed to "love" me. In fact, when my husband came along, back at the university, it took me time and some conscious effort to relax a little and open to being friends with him.

Much like my final year in the university where I had to survive on friends, one of my most embarrassing and depressing years growing up was my third year in Junior Secondary School, second and third term to be precise. Throughout both of those terms, I sat by the school gate on every visiting day with anticipation and desperate hope to see someone – anybody – from my home walk in through the school gate. And how so disappointed I felt every single time. No one showed up.

Literally, I had *nothing*. No edible provision, no bathing or washing soap, no toothpaste, no body cream, *nothing*. And, you may recall that my clothes were in bad shape and my shoes worn out. I might have easily passed as the poorest girl in school – or at least one of them. And some students repeatedly mocked me, while a few others sympathized.

I utilized every opportunity I got to send messages of my plight home, but all my messages fell on deaf ears. I sent day students or sick students going home who lived near my house, yet no response. No one visited. And to worsen my situation, my junior WAEC exam was to commence and I had no writing materials – pencil, pen, mathematical set, colour paints, etc. I was simply a girl getting by every day. In the first place, I had resumed school at the beginning of the term with very scarce provision and a promise to be visited with much more and some money. That was it. I learned to just survive and quit waiting on them. I recall that I had to go into the examination hall with about 6 discarded pens with their ink nearly finished that I picked on the floor around the school area. And I had to beg the invigilators to permit me to request necessary items during the exam and I was granted.

Interestingly, during this period of arduous and excruciating wait, one of my aunts came to visit another student that she knew somehow and brought her all manner of provisions. Unknown to her, the girl she visited, who was a senior in SS3, was my school mother. So, my school mother was excited for me, thinking I finally got to be visited. Then she asked me about it, but I told her I didn't know what she was talking about. She was shocked and told me that my aunt had just left the school and showed me the things she was given. I couldn't say a word; I just let it pass. Already, I had received enough mockery from asking for practically everything for months. And when it became too much, I started to trade my meat or fish from the dining hall for most of these items that I needed. I was practically being conditioned to survive no matter what. Sometimes I got so emotional and wept to myself.

On one of the days when I got so emotional, I decided to take a walk. And as I walked, I was looking up to the skies and questioning the only person I thought I could question – God. I asked God, *"Why me?"* *"Is it not better I go back to my mum who doesn't even know what is going on with me over here in Lagos?"* I uttered. Then a scripture came to my mind; I believed it was God answering me. It was Jeremiah 1:5-6.

"Before I formed you in the womb, I knew you; before you were born, I sanctified you; I ordained you a prophet to the nations." Then said I: "Ah, Lord God! Behold, I cannot speak, for I am a youth."

At the time, I knew very little about God since meeting Him in my first year in school. Yet He was saying He knew me. So then, why did He allow these happenings in my life? How can you say before I was born you knew me, yet so many tragedies came by under your watch? You see, I didn't know better. I blamed God for just everything because He was the one I believed could listen with understanding and not threaten me. And at that point in my life, my understanding of God was that he was the Creator of all things and my source, full stop. I suppose that what He was trying to make me see, which my young mind couldn't fathom at the time, is that my voice, which stems from my identity, was the devil's target. The devil wanted to silence me so I would not be able to accomplish God's intent for my life. The best way for him to do that was to assault my understanding of who I was – my identity!

What caught my attention in the portion of scripture above was the word, 'speak'; it stood out to me. By this time, I didn't have a voice, remember? I was afraid to make my opinion known anywhere. I couldn't express hate or love; I was wondering who I was and whose daughter I was. I battled with a **high** level of **low** self-esteem, facing rejection, humiliation and hunger. Yet, here was God seeming to say I have a voice to speak to nations. Was he joking or something?

Well, that got me even more confused, especially since none of the things happening to me seemed to suggest that God knew what He was saying. So, I questioned Him for what He really meant by those words, but I got no answers. I would later in life come to understand.

Similar to Esther, this was my "Mordecai" saying you are important, you are loved, you have a relationship with Me, your identity is intact in Me, you have value, you are accepted, you are not a mistake, you have a voice and a purpose; speak up! Esther had influence and favour with the king, which she was not aware of or didn't believe was bigger than her fear of the laws and customs of the Persian Empire. She needed the prodding of Mordecai to exercise this influence. Likewise, I had an identity in Christ, which was there long before I realized it. It was there already. It was my identity; I only needed to see it and exercise it. I only needed an understanding of who I am to regain my voice. And thank God I did!

Recall what Mordecai said to Esther: "*For if you REMAIN SILENT at this time* " In other words, Mordecai had noticed that Esther's voice towards her assignment had been silent for some time, but now, she needed to *speak up* more than ever before.

Writing this book, for me, is proof that I am not ready to remain on the mat. Nothing will keep me bound with self-pity and depression. I am going all out to do and say what I am instructed. I am certain that someone reading this now may need to find their voice. Someone needs to rise above the situations and circumstances that life has thrown in their path and refuse to allow the devil to use the circumstances of their past to keep them silent. Finding your voice is not just about your vocal undulations or the act of talking. It is about you stepping up, stepping out, and taking the actions necessary to bring you into the place of your dominance. Standing up for your passion, giving expression to the vision that for so long has laid dormant and burdened your heart.

You have been silent for too long on your assignment and haven't really stepped into your domain of authority in God - to evangelize, to speak up for the less privileged and for abused people, to make provision for widows and orphans, to serve the body of Christ in specific ways, to speak to people with specific problems for which you have been empowered with the solution. What community, society, organization or people are you supposed to be a solution to? Many books, songs and life experiences are still locked up inside you. It's time to open your mouth and speak as God has empowered you and step into your place of dominance. It is time to step up to that fear, like I did the bully and this book. It is time to call the bluff of the devil. Do not allow the devil to keep you silent, else like Mordecai said to Esther, God will raise salvation for the people without you and you may lose your significance. God forbids!

How to Discover Your Domain of Authority

1.   *Yield to the Holy Spirit*

The Holy Spirit's witness in your heart is the ultimate guide to knowing God's precise assignment for your life, which He communicates to you as you fellowship with Him. Knowing God's purpose for your life and being guided by the Holy Spirit to fulfil it is a great leap. Yield to the

Holy Spirit. Let Him reveal to you the mind of the Father concerning your life. He alone knows your mission here on earth, and the details needed to work it out. The more you yield to Him, the more He inspires and empowers you to fulfil your mandate.

2.   Past Experiences

It is not cast in stone, but many times our experiences show us what we were born to do. That is, what you suffered and conquered can be a pointer to your assignment, which can be to help other people suffering similar ordeals. To help them escape and conquer like you did. As a personal example, I currently run an NGO that was largely inspired by my experiences with lack as a child. Love for humanity has always been a part of me. Again, I believe that was born from the lack and pain I went through as a child. I always feel a deep sense of empathy when I encounter people in need. Sometimes, I wish I could help everyone, but of course I can't. There is only so much that I can do.

By God's grace we have been able to do more in the lives of people, especially widows, fatherless children, and the less privileged in different communities. God used my past experiences of lack and want to point me towards an assignment He wants me to undertake.

3.   Passion

What are you passionate about? What makes you tick? What do you love and enjoy doing with ease? It could be a pointer. Search your heart to find it. Then allow the Holy Spirit direct you on what He wants you to channel your attention and energy towards. Thereafter, take necessary actions based on what He tells you. Learn to invest in your passion, to improve. Do not be satisfied with where you are. Let your passion drive you to aim higher.

4. *Self-Awareness*

This closely relates to the former point. The more aware you are of yourself, the more you can identify your passion, strengths, weaknesses, interests, talents, skills, etc. These can also point you towards your assignment in tandem with the witness of the Spirit in your heart.

5. *Feedback*

Sometimes, seek to get feedback from people around you who love and care for you enough to be open and straight with you. Ask them what they think your key areas of strengths are and what you do most easily. Once you get their feedback, run it by what you know about yourself and check with your heart for ultimate direction.

Chapter

SEVEN

HER LEGACY

The word 'legacy' is not common in most people's vocabularies. It is not a term you would hear often. Maybe that is because it seems to suggest coming close to the end of one's life (a wrong presumption). Something many of us hate to hear or think about. Nevertheless, whether you like to hear it or not, it is inevitable that you and I must depart from this earth into eternity someday. Hence, it is greatly important to live intentionally, to live with a heart pouring with love for others.

For David, after he had served his own generation by the
will of God, fell asleep
– Act 13:36

Often, as people begin to age, they begin to think about what their legacy will be. It is perhaps late by then, but it is certainly not timely to only begin thinking of legacy then. Simply put, your legacy is what you want to be remembered for. And what you should be remembered for is how you served your generation in accordance with God's will for your life– your assignment. Therefore, we talked about your domain in chapter 6.

As the King's heir, your legacy wouldn't be an issue if you truly exercise dominion in your domain. In other words, your legacy starts from this moment, regardless of how young or old you are. The memories you will leave in the lives of the people that you touch and impact by how you live now will be the culmination of your legacy. This therefore shows that the concept of leaving a legacy is not a distant idea or notion that is to be put off until one starts to draw nearer to one's grave. No! Your legacy starts now and builds up throughout your life. Your legacy will be the summation of the lives you impacted during your lifetime. It will be the summarized version of how you lived out God's purpose for your life here on earth.

From the day you received Jesus into your life and became His beloved daughter and He changed you, your legacy to your world started; because from the instant you were changed, purpose was activated inside you. And living out your purpose is building up your life's legacy.

Ambassador of the King

This is where it all starts. Knowing that you have been made the King's heir and empowered for good works, God expects you to live as His representative on earth, to cause others to see Him, know Him and come to Him through you. God expects you to live your life as an ambassador of heaven here on earth. And when you do, that is enough legacy.

An ambassador is an emissary whose job is to represent, convey and defend the interests of his or her home country in the land of their deployment. Ambassadors maintain constant connection with their home country and translates their stance on issues to the host country.

This is what our King-Father expects of you and me. He wants us to maintain constant fellowship with Him so that we can learn of His ways and represent them to our world, causing them to see our light and thereby glorify God.

Your legacy doesn't have to be to the whole world, but to the people and the lives that you encounter every day. What will your organization say about you after you exit? Or your children, how is your life influencing them? How about your immediate residential, religious or social communities, what will they remember of you when your time here elapses? Your relatives and friends, what would their testimony of your life be? That you did the will of your Father is enough legacy. You only need to find out what His will is for your life and occupy yourself with living it out. Make yourself valuable to someone around you, someone who needs your help and impact. Building your legacy starts with a simple commitment to serving other people.

Our Assignment as His Ambassadors
As believers, the great commission to go into all the world and touch lives should be our greatest ambition on earth. You cannot live an ordinary life when an extraordinary God inhabits you. The Bible says we are the salt of the earth. And we know that salt is useless unless applied. For salt to be relevant to anyone or anything it must first meet a need. Salt has qualities such as to preserve, to disinfect and to sanitize. So, for the Bible to say that we are the salt of the earth, it means that the world is in need of salt because of its qualities. The earnest expectation of creation waits for the manifestation of the sons of God. The application of the salt is our uniqueness.

Gross darkness fills the earth, but we are told to rise and shine amid the darkness and spread the light of comfort, peace and love. In the same light, when love, peace, joy, comfort, healing is lacking in a family, community or nation, you will know. Can you imagine how the world would be if every one of us radiates our light and apply our taste? There would be a tremendous manifestation of the glory of God.

Our bodies are the temple of the living God. "Do you not know that you yourselves are God's temple, and that God's Spirit dwells in you?" (1 Corinthians 3:16). This is to say, we are carriers of His glory. We are transporters, moving Him to wherever He desires to enter. We are the vessels that He resides in to go into nations, families, educational institutions, government parastatals, media houses, and into every sphere of the society and churches.

God does not dwell in a house built with hands; we are His dwelling place, the place of His abode. He desires that we live our lives like people who are conscious of the fact that they are carrying His presence. We do not need to travel far to consult with God, He indwells us every second of the day. The world doesn't need to see God for them to believe that He exists. Seeing us most times is the only God they need. We are the God they see. When we appear, God appears. Glory!

Essential Tool for Building a Legacy

You can only build a legacy with one key ingredient: *love*. Loving yourself and others is very essential. You must love yourself first, and then love others. If you don't love yourself, you will limit yourself; and by limiting yourself you cannot show affection to others. Until you give yourself to a great cause funded by love and compassion, you haven't really begun to fully live. As I write about self-love, I am amused by the fact that I can be doing so. Isn't God just too wonderful? Who could have imagined that this would be possible for me? Certainly not me! But the great King, the One who creates possibilities out of impossibilities, saw past my predicaments, reached deep inside me and changed my heart of self-hatred and self-disgust into one that can now give rich love to others. Wow! Thank You Jesus!

As I've shared before, my experiences in the past made me develop a debilitating low self-esteem and I lost all confidence to the point that every time anyone, including my husband, complimented me, I would interpret it as an insincere attempt to take advantage of me.

I felt rejection palpably. I never believed in myself or in my mind. I was abjectly inadequate and unwanted. I lost my vocal confidence. I lost every bit of likeness for myself, let alone love. There were days I even wanted to take my life, as I had stated several times in this book, but I somehow never got around to attempting it. Sometimes, for protracted periods, I lived in perpetual depression. I never believed I was worth anything. I lost a lot of opportunities because of low self-esteem and feelings of inadequacy. But look at me today; because of my King-Father, I am a blessing to many around me, not only to my immediate family. I have a thriving business with happy staff members, and I am involved with different community impact initiatives and ministries that reach out to hundreds of people to bless them. Only the King could make that happen!

Channels of Mercy

Serving as God's healing hand to the hurting world should be paramount in our hearts. We should seek to administer relief to men both physically and spiritually. We should release the balm of Gilead to heal the hurt of many. We should gather the outcast for the Lord. Liberate the oppressed. Set the captives free. Take care of the destitute.

One thing of major significance to God is the wellbeing of the poor, the needy and the oppressed. He is very much interested in their case. We should be an embodiment of solutions and a channel of extending God's mercy to them. *"Whoever oppresses the poor shows contempt for their Maker, but whoever is kind to the needy honours God"* (Proverbs 13:31).

Many nations are hurting. Some are in pains as a result of cold wars, natural disasters like floods, earthquakes, bush fires, etc. Citizens are crying out for help. We have a responsibility to make ourselves readily available to the Lord to be sent to these nations as an extension of His hand to release healing unto them and bring an end to their hurt and pain. Apart from nations that are in pain, around us are individuals, families, cities, communities and churches still languishing in afflictions. We are to minister healing to their wounds.

Jesus is the best gift any one can receive, and He is the best gift we can give anyone. The Bible says God desires all men to be saved and to come to the knowledge of truth. We see here that salvation of souls and the revelation of God's word is God's ultimate desire for humanity. If we are faithful ambassadors and we are after what pleases Him, we will make sure we carry out our assignment at all cost. We were commanded to "go into the world and make disciples of all nations," (Matt. 28:19) and go we must, for everything we need to fulfil our assignment has been given to us in the person of the Holy Spirit. Without Him there is little we can do for the Kingdom.

Pathway to Greatness

"Not all of us can do great things. But we can do small things with great love."
- Mother Teresa

Every time I think about the concept of legacy, one person that readily comes to mind is Mother Teresa. She is an epitome of selflessness and service to humanity. She lived her life convinced of what she was called to do and poured herself wholly to it, even at times when it was most inconvenient. She sacrificed literally everything for the good and wellbeing of others, especially the poor and downtrodden of society – people who were deprived of love, care, attention and dignity.

Mother Teresa realized early what she wanted her life to be about. She wanted to be a nun and serve poor people. So, she enrolled to become a nun at age 18. Then, once she had completed her training and had been inducted in Ireland, she was sent to Calcutta in India to serve. Once there, she started off as a classroom teacher, but soon left that to serve the many poor people she saw in her community, propelled by her passion. She founded a small organization called The Missionaries of Charity to cater for the needs of the poor and dying. She committed wholly to it and got few other nuns to join her cause. And, as the number of people they were serving started to grow, they left the convent and chose rather to live among the poor people they were serving. Consequently, they had to live on very meagre income and resources, while still sharing with the poor; until their work started to get noticed by some Indian politicians and well-meaning individuals in the society – and later the entire world.

Mother Teresa's actions were driven by love for humanity. She said, *"Love cannot remain by itself – it has no meaning. Love has to be put into action, and that action is service."* How true! Beyond Mother Teresa's example, every person who has truly left a lasting impact and legacy in our world has always been compelled to service by love. Service is the pathway to attaining true greatness. And love must be the fuel. Jesus said, *" whoever desires to be great among you, let him be your servant. And whoever desires to be first among you, let him be your slave"* (Matthew 20:26-27). Philosopher and Nobel Peace Prize winner Albert Schweitzer corroborated this by saying, *"I don't know what your destiny will be, but one thing I know: the only ones among you who will be really happy are those who have sought and found how to serve."*

Mother Teresa was sold out to serving the poor so much that when, in 1979, she was awarded the Nobel Peace Prize, she did not attend the ceremonial banquet, but requested that the $192,000 prize money be given to the poor. Even when in the last two decades of her life she suffered poor, deteriorating health, she never refrained from travelling around the world to the different countries where her mission projects were represented. She was sold out to her cause, backed by the infinite power of love. Is it any wonder that the humble organization she started in the 1930s in Calcutta, India is still alive and active today, and now operating in over 130 countries? She lived full and died empty, having poured out all she was loaded with by her Maker to dispense to her world. She left a legacy, and the world is yet to recover from it because she loved in truth and then served.

Other exemplary lives to emulate are:
1. Deborah: Deborah was one of the first female prophetesses in Israel. She was a wife and had the responsibilities of managing a home with all

the challenges associated with it. Yet, Deborah knew who she was; she knew her purpose in life.

When you know who you are, it gives you focus and direction in life. Note that Deborah arose to answer God's call upon her life in a season when women were treated as lesser breeds, a season when women could not sit in the same gathering as men; when women were not allowed to talk where men did; a season when women were neither recognized nor given political positions. She is an encouragement to women in all ramifications and facets. When we feel ignored, mistreated or overlooked, we can gain stability by looking at Deborah's life. Her wisdom in administering justice to the people, her military strategy, bravery, inner strength, ability to hear God, willingness to be used by God, her faith in God and calm leadership are worth emulating.

2. Huldah: Huldah was the wife of Shallum, the keeper of the royal wardrobe. She is another prophetess that God raised in her time to bring sanity back to the land. She was well known for her spiritual discernment and piety. Amid lawlessness and idolatry, a woman, God's prophetess, held on and was able to bring forth the word of the Lord that generated a significant religious reformation. She was a woman of prayer and God's mouthpiece. Although Israel was lost in idolatry and in bondage to gods that were not God, Huldah did not mince words in releasing the prophetic word for the season to those who needed to hear them. She spoke accurately, clearly and sharply when she was needed to interpret the prophecy of the scroll found in the temple. She had the prophetic word of the hour and she spoke it as God's messenger with boldness, even to the king. She was not afraid of the consequences of her actions because she knew she heard from God. 2nd Chronicles 34:14-33.

3. Harriet Tubman: She was a black slave woman who helped to free many other slaves by her courage. She was small in stature, but she had the heart of a lioness. Tubman was an illiterate. She lived alone and often took up employment as house help to earn enough money to enable her smuggle slaves through an underground rail route. She also worked occasionally in small hotels cooking and scrubbing floors. She would disappear from her workplace only to appear again. Her employers did not know where she disappeared to and what she did while she was away. In 1857, she redeemed 300 slaves through a secret rail tunnel. Her inability to read and write did not deter her. She was a woman of courage and confidence.

4. Aimee Semple-McPherson was a Pentecostal pioneer. At a time when men were in the forefront of ministry, she became a trailblazer, a model for both men and women. She built the 5000-seater Angelus Temple.

In July 1922, she started one of the fastest growing denominations today – the Four-square Gospel Church. Aimee Semple-McPherson was the first Pentecostal minister to preach on radio. She started the first Christian radio in the United States. She also pioneered the Life Bible College where 8000 ministers were trained before her death in 1944. She composed about 175 songs and hymns, wrote 13 dramas and many operas. Between 1917 and 1923, Aimee preached in more than 100 counties in the US. Between 1919 and 1923, she travelled across the length and breadth of the country.

5. Amanda Smith: Amanda was a slave. She did not have the opportunity to go to school, so she taught herself how to read and write. She worked as a cook and a washerwoman. Her diligence can be seen from the fact that she worked hard to support her child after her husband died in the American civil war. Prayer and praise were her way of life. Amanda Smith served God with her beautiful voice, singing and preaching in England, Scotland, India, America and Africa.

As an intercessor, she organized men and women to pray in groups. She was a woman of great compassion. She founded the Amanda Smith American Children Foundation. Amanda Smith adopted two African children when she came to Africa. She was a woman of deep consecration. Her motto was "Without holiness, no man shall see the Lord."

There are many great men and women of God who He has anointed to make more positive impact in their world. You are one of them. You cannot allow yourself to be intimidated. Pursue the vision God has put in your heart with passion. Be willing to give your life for it if it comes to that. Put in all that you have to that pursuit. You cannot afford to leave your world the same way you met it. It is not the number of years that you live that matters to God, it is how much you gave to your world. How many people have had their destinies and lives turned around because of you? How will your world remember you after you are gone? What legacy are you leaving behind? God has blessed you with His very life to make a difference. Sow your talents, skills, potentials, money and properties into the kingdom. Use it to touch and save lives and ensure that people leave you better than how they were when they met you.

The one whose life you are living should ultimately define your vision and purpose on earth. The bible says, "It is no longer I who live, but Christ lives in me" so therefore Christ's desires should be what consumes you, which is to have all men saved and to come to the knowledge of the truth.

God is looking for people who have discovered their identities in Christ Jesus and are ready to reach out to the whole world with the gospel of truth. He seeks people whose pockets are open to this mission – people whose heart's sleeping and waking thoughts belong to this mission. God is looking for people who are so passionate to fulfil their purpose on earth that they can lay down their lives for it. They do not succumb to the status quo.

You are that change agent that your family, community, city and nation have been waiting for. You are the one to reintroduce Christ to your world and to recover the grounds that the global church has lost over the years. While you have delayed over the years, so many souls tied to your loins have gone to eternity without Jesus. Maybe you are waiting to have all physical things put together before fulfilling the purpose of God for creating you. It shouldn't be; you already have all that it takes – the life of Christ.

The great harvest cannot be gathered without you. This is not the day you are to remain hidden in obscurity, in a closet, behind others and lying on the mat. It is a new day when you must rise and shine. Awake to your reality and begin to release yourself into all the earth. God has used seemingly weak and feeble people to do great and mighty things.

Your limitation lies in your mind. You are who you know you are. When you discover who you are and what you are capable of, you will gain more confidence for impact. There is no weakness that God cannot turn into strength. There is no disadvantage that God cannot turn into an advantage. Everyone has something beautiful to offer to his or her generation. There is a diamond encased in your disability. There is a pearl concealed in your pain. You too can be a woman or man of commitment and consistency. There is greatness resident in you.

Steps to Living Life to the Fullest

1.   Renew your mind with the word of God

Allow God's word to wash your mind. "And do not be conformed to this world, but be transformed by the renewing of your mind, that you may prove what *is* that good and acceptable and perfect will of God" (Romans 12:2). Confess God's word about yourself until it is your firm belief; until you can sincerely say you are what God's word declares you are. You are born of the word; identify with the word of God. You are not what happened to you, so you can't be defined by it.

2.   Pray and fellowship with the Holy Spirit

Man was created with the need for divinity. No matter how people claim not to believe in God, deep down there is a hunger for Him inside them. This world is broken chiefly because it does not believe in the only One that heals every brokenness. No relationship you get into will heal you. No amount of wealth will heal you. Tell God everything and ask Him to direct you on what you need to do and who you need to talk to about what you have been going through. To make physical impact on people, you must contact divinity with your prayers. Build up your most holy faith praying in the Holy Ghost (Jude 20).

3. *Guard your heart with all diligence*

This is the very crux of the matter, a very important part of your healing process. What happened to you in the past got to you and instantly made you feel unloved, unwanted and unappreciated, but if we learn to guard what we watch, what we hear, and who we talk to, we will get back our liberty for good.

4. *Get support pillars*

There are people you can learn from by being around them, watching them closely and achieving the same results you see them achieve. A coach is someone you hire to walk you through your life goals and help you achieve them. He or she is all about making you the best you can be.

Mentors, on the other hand, are people who have your best interest at heart. You can have mentors at different points of your life. A mentor is someone you can ask about anything and they would give you feedback based on what they have experienced. Look for the person that is doing something that you would love to do, both far and near. If they are far, get their materials; they can do a lot in your life. The ones that are near, you can easily access and ask them questions often.

5. *Engage in helping others*

Don't bypass an opportunity to help someone. Develop an intentional attitude of asking questions and talking to people. You never know what challenges people are facing. Remember again the lady I told you about previously who said she didn't believe in the existence of God. Unlike the former me who would not have spoken to her because of my insecurities, I went up to her that day to talk and keep her company while she did her hair. And after our conversation that day and I prayed for her, I stayed on her case, checking up on her periodically, till she gave birth to her lovely twins.

There are many people going through challenging situations and are hoping that someone will come around and talk to them. God is counting on you. Don't allow their countenance intimidate you. If only you knew what is behind that facade!

6. Get involved

The life God has given you is yours and you do not get another opportunity to live it. This is the chance you get to live your life the way He designed for you to live it. Get excited about the things you have and look forward with excitement to the endless possibilities God can bring you into.

Getting involved with activities that make you happy has a way of helping your mind to achieve better. The last thing you want is to be idle or feel sorry for yourself when you can make the most of your life. The world is already full of people who are not happy with their results, people who continue to sit in a place and do the same things over again and are bewildered that they continue to get the same results. Choose to surrender your pain to God and decide to put a smile on someone else's face every day.

You don't know what is on the other side of your obedience. People are waiting to be saved, get delivered and be healed. You can't afford to be lying by the pool when someone's life depends on your living fully. Someone's next breath depends on your choice to be everything God has planned for you to be. Live out all your possibilities. Venture out to help and encourage younger adults. Inspire other women and men to do more and achieve more with their lives. I will never stop what I am doing because someone hurt me, neither should you.

7. *Develop self confidence*

The ability to believe in yourself can change your life. We have been conditioned throughout our lives to doubt ourselves. We must retrain ourselves to get rid of our fears and self-doubt in order to build self-esteem and self-confidence. Recognize your ability to accomplish goals. Be optimistic about the future as you set goals and achieve them.

The support of others will benefit you, but it is you who must make the changes necessary for you to start believing in yourself. Sometimes, your difficulties in believing in yourself can stem from the fact that you haven't really given yourself anything to believe in. When you develop a clear vision for what you want, start developing strategies for realizing that vision and start achieving small goals along the way. With that, you increase your self-belief, one small step at a time.

No one can make you feel inferior without your consent. Whatever you call yourself is what others will call you. Believe in the person God has made you to be. Love yourself so much that everyone that comes into your life will invariably love you the way you love yourself.

Low self-confidence is not a life sentence. Self-confidence can be learnt, practiced and mastered just like any other skill. And once you master it, everything in your life will change for the better.

Building Your Legacy

In conclusion, as we have established already, your legacy starts with the discovery of who you are in Christ – your identity – and committing to be a blessing to other people. Your past pain should not go to waste. Draw strength from it to meet the needs of other people who might be going through the same.

The Bible says that Jesus is a competent High Priest for us because He can be touched by the feelings of our weaknesses. *"For we do not have a High Priest who cannot sympathize with our weaknesses, but was in all points tempted as we are, yet without sin"* (Hebrews 4:15). He walked the earth and experienced the very challenges that befall us, so He can readily identify with us. Likewise, your pain of the past and the eventual victories brought you to this point where you can easily relate with the plight of anyone going through the same or similar troubles. So, God brings them in contact with you so that you can help them to overcome, as He helped you too. Don't neglect such opportunities. Always remember that you are blessed to be a blessing.

This is the simple pathway to building a legacy that will outlive you because any person whose life becomes better through your touch of love will never forget you. You will live in their hearts for as long as they live.

I trust God that this book has been of tremendous blessing to you. Now imagine if I had not taken the step of obedience to share my story with you to help you find hope and succour from your own hurt. Our pain, once we have overcome, should serve God's purpose for our lives – to help better other people's lives.

And the Lord said, "Simon, Simon! Indeed, Satan has asked for you, that he may sift you as wheat. But I have prayed for you, that your faith should not fail; and WHEN YOU HAVE RETURNED TO ME, STRENGTHEN YOUR BRETHREN."
– Luke 22:31-32 (emphasis mine)

This is the summary of why God healed you from your past pain and hurts. Don't let them lie in waste. Go out and help another to heal and to find their true, unbroken identity in Christ. Building a legacy is a product of consistency. Be consistent at it.

Remain in and bask in the King's love always.

I love and celebrate you.

Never forget: *You are the King's heir!*

REFERENCES

Chapter 1

1. http://fathers.com/statistics-and-research/the-extent-of-fatherlessness/
2. https://www.npr.org/sections/ed/2017/06/18/533062607/poverty-dropouts-pregnancy-suicide-what-the-numbers-say-about-fatherless-kids
3. https://www.fatherhood.org/father-absence-statistic
4. https://onlinenigeria.com/columnists/ad.php?blurb=645
5. http://feminine.com.ng/2019/01/11/how-absent-fathers-are-hurting-their-children/
6. https://www.pediatricsoffranklin.com/resources-and-education/pediatric-care/the-importance-of-a-father-in-a-childs-life/
7. https://www.pediatricsoffranklin.com/resources-and-education/pediatric-care/the-importance-of-a-father-in-a-childs-life/

Chapter 3

1. https://warifng.org/rape-stats-in-nigeria/

ALSO AVAILABLE ON E-BOOK

Download Now: www.beckyibrahim.com

The tears, trials and triumph of the King's daughter

In this book, the author takes a nosedive into the sea of vulnerability to share her story of how life broke her hard, in her earliest years through to adulthood, and left her wondering who she was and why she had to endure all of those pains and heartaches. Hers was a long streak of tumultuous, unstable and traumatic childhood experiences, which saw her lose all sense of worth, esteem and confidence in herself. The thrust of this book is to practically show you that irrespective of what crippling circumstances life has doled you – whether in the past or present, you are the King's heir, and your identity in Him is still intact. Your circumstances in life are not the determinants of your identity, but who the King – your Father – says you are. As such, no matter what your past or present says or looks like, you have an unbroken identity in Christ! This book is solely intended to reveal to you, or remind you, who you are – whole and complete in Him.

This book will take you through a journey of self-discovery and a fulfilling life in Christ hereafter. It is a tool that the Holy Spirit will use to bring healing to your heart and give you a peek into His divine call upon your life. He will also empower you to become that mighty woman or man of valour who will confront and defeat the oppressors of your life, your family's, your community's and the many destinies God has tied to yours.

the author

BECKY IBRAHIM, the King's daughter, is a lover of Christ. The CEO of Pwatee's Beautique Salon and Spa. She is passionate about helping women and young adults live freely and fully and to their best potential. Her vision is to inspire and empower the downtrodden, deprived and stigmatized, so they can heal and become independent, discovering all they were born to be.
She has been married to her adorable husband Akeem Ibrahim for 13 years. They are blessed with 3 awesome boys.

ISBN 978-978-983-296-5